STRANGE
ANGELS

&

OTHER PLAYS

SCOTT DOUGLAS

STRANGE ANGELS

& OTHER PLAYS

WOOD LAKE BOOKS

Editor: Michael Schwartzentruber
Cover and interior design: Margaret Kyle
Proofreader: Dianne Greenslade

Back cover photo of Scott Douglas: Andrew Douglas
Front cover photos: Donna Sinclair, Richard Choe,
    and Nanette McKay

We acknowledge the financial support of
the Government of Canada through the Book Publishing
Industry Development Program (BPIDP) for our
publishing activities.

At Wood Lake Books, we practice what we publish, guided
by a concern of fairness, justice, and equal opportunity in
all of our relationships with employees and customers.

We recycle and reuse and encourage readers to do the
same. Resources are printed on recycled paper and
more environmentally friendly groundwood papers
(newsprint) whenever possible. The trees used are
replaced through donations to the Scoutrees for Canada
program. A portion of all profits is donated to charitable
organizations.

National Library of Canada Cataloguing in Publication
Douglas, Scott, 1969–
    Strange angels & other plays/Scott Douglas.
ISBN 1-55145-499-8
    I. Title.
PS8557.O812335S87 2004   C812'.6   C2004-900104-3

PERFORMANCE RIGHTS: for information about
royalties and permission to perform the plays in this book
e-mail Scott Douglas at: **scottdouglas@woodlake.com**

Published by
WOOD LAKE BOOKS INC.
9025 Jim Bailey Road
Kelowna, British Columbia
Canada V4V 1R2

250.766.2778
info@woodlake.com
www.joinhands.com
www.woodlake.com

Printing 10 9 8 7 6 5 4 3 2 1

Printed in Canada
by
Quebecor, Edmonton, AB

TABLE OF CONTENTS

INTRODUCTION

PLAYS

APPENDIX

ACKNOWLEDGMENTS

Many of these plays were commissioned works. Thank you to the various groups and committees that asked me to give them a play: the United Church 75th Anniversary committee, the United Church Division of Ministry Personnel and Education, the Social Justice committee of Saskatchewan Conference, various committees in Manitoba and Northwestern Ontario Conference, Allison Rennie and the organizers of the British Columbia Youth Conference, Ten Days for Global Justice, and St. Andrew's College in Saskatoon. Thank you for encouraging my work and for giving my plays a forum.

I also wish to acknowledge all the actors who have performed these plays over the years, especially the actors of the "Quatro" group in British Columbia and the "Money-Joy-Church" troupe from Winnipeg. These actors road-tested and molded many of these plays, and part of the fun of writing was trying to create parts that would match the creativity and talent of these great performers and friends.

Thank you to my family for support and encouragement, to Ted Dodd for inspiration and example, and to Nanette McKay for being with me every step of the way (advising, challenging, making puppets, covering her eyes while I dove off ladders or walked on stilts, tolerating my obsessive hours sitting at the computer talking to myself, and for being a simply wonderful person).

And thank you to all the enthusiastic, receptive audiences who have enjoyed these plays and encouraged the writing of more.

INTRODUCTION

A warning against the use of drama in church

Hopefully, you will enjoy this collection of plays written for various church communities over the last ten years. They might even inspire you to bring drama into your own church context.

Let me be the first to warn you against such a foolish course of action!

The Early Church Fathers – wise leaders of the early Christian community that they were – clearly denounced the inclusion of anything that even smacked of theater in worship. According to them, theater was sinful, immoral, idolatrous, pagan, and dangerous!

The Early Church Fathers knew whereof they spoke. Drama is dangerous stuff.

For one thing, drama undermines authority. You see, no one character in a play gets to tell the whole story. That's the definition of a drama; it's a story told in *many* voices. Rather than expressing an authoritative once-and-for-all Truth, drama holds up many competing truths. A variety of perspectives. The result is an image of reality that can be complex, maybe even ambiguous. When plays such as the ones in this collection are done well, they start conversations, or even debates. So if you're looking for a medium that will help you say, "This is how it is!" with absolute certainty and all the right answers, drama is not your friend.

Drama has a tendency to shake things up. For example, when I'm working with a group of actors who are going to present a drama in a church sanctuary, one of the first things I ask them to do is "claim the space." This means wandering around, lying on the floor, climbing over and under pews, curling up under the Communion table, banging on the piano, running, jumping, shouting, looking behind curtains and doors – in other words, doing all the things your parents told you *not* to do as a child because the church is a "sacred space" where you should sit quietly and try not to touch anything. But good theater refuses to sit quietly. So when I'm working on a drama, I need actors to feel comfortable enough to *play*. Sometimes this means shaking up some firmly held (and often unconscious) assumptions. What starts off as a re-evaluation of our sense of space usually ends up as a re-thinking of deeper assumptions about what is "appropriate," "respectful," and "holy." Now we're getting into dangerous territory, right?

Finally, drama invites conflict. Rather than seeing conflict as something to be feared and avoided, drama claims conflict as energy. Who's right? Who's wrong? Who's going to win? Who am I cheering for? Where do I stand? Conflict gets our juices pumping. It pulls us to the edge of our seats. If it's done well, drama can pull us out of our comfort zones. It can make us see something we didn't expect to see. It can pick us up and take us on a journey. Sometimes the journey is gentle, initiated with a chuckle or a smile. Sometimes the journey is frightening, disorienting, or infuriating. Whatever kind of trip it is, we end up in a different place than we started. In other words, drama – when it connects with us – has the power to transform.

And maybe we don't want to be transformed. Maybe the church doesn't want to be transformed.

And that's why drama is dangerous.

On the other hand, maybe the church is hungry for transformation. (In the same way that the theater is hungry for community and a sense of spiritual connectedness.) Maybe the church is willing to embrace complexity, ambiguity, diversity, and conflict.

Maybe the church is ready to play.

Some of the plays in this collection are challenging. Some are comforting. Some will invite you to laugh at yourself, some will invite you to think about things in a different way, some will invite you to take risks, some will invite you to argue with characters and their ideas. Some will just invite you to have fun.

If you are willing to take the risk, then welcome to this book.

Just don't say I didn't warn you.

The Plays

Strange Angels was first performed for a meeting of Manitoba and Northwestern Ontario Conference in 1997, for a theme entitled "Strangers and Other Angels." Partly inspired by a series of Bob Haverluck cartoons, it is a story about a normal middle-class man who encounters a stranger who defies categorization. He may be a mentally-ill bum, or an angel, or both.

Dog Eat Dog World is a "little puppet play for big children" introducing the concept of poor bashing. It was first performed for a meeting of Saskatchewan Conference in 1998 at the request of the Social Justice Committee. In the original production, it was performed by actors with dog and cat puppets. It has also been performed by actors in dog and cat make-up and masks. (It has yet to be performed by actual dogs and cats.)

A Fair Trade was first published by Ten Days for Global Justice in 1998 as part of a worship resource package. It is the story of a perplexed Canadian woman who discovers a Nicaraguan coffee farmer in her kitchen, and a befuddled Canadian man who wakes up to find himself trying to make a living growing coffee beans.

David's Rule is a revisionist version of the biblical King David saga told from the perspective of David's fictional little sister, Hannah. It was written in 1992 for a British Columbia youth conference on the theme of rules and authority. It was originally performed in five parts over the course of a weekend.

Work is a reflection on employment and unemployment, especially as it affects young people. It mixes job interview monologues with stylized movement. The monologues are largely based on the experiences of the 20-something actors in the Money-Joy-Church theater troupe, who also performed it in 1997 for a meeting of Manitoba and Northwestern Ontario Conference.

Just 'Cause was written at the request of a committee in Manitoba that ended up calling itself the "Beyond Family Values" group, and was performed in 1999. It is an exploration of the institution of marriage and of the definition of "family," from the perspective of a doubt-ridden bride and a highly invested mother. (My mom doesn't think I gave the mother in this play enough good arguments, and she's probably right. My guess, though, is that in most contexts the mother will get more sympathy from the audience.)

Legend of Saint Andrew is written in the style of the medieval miracle (or saint) plays. It is based on actual legends and stories told about St. Andrew. The relationship between the gruff and abrasive St. Andrew and the timid St. Matthias also presents a parable of the contemporary church and its approach to ministry and mission. The play was first performed in 1996 at St. Andrew's College United Church theological school in Saskatoon, by the Money-Joy-Church theater troupe (who drove through a blizzard from Winnipeg to present it!).

Tables Turned and the Stone Gets Rolled Away is an Easter play written in 1994. The characters in the play are simultaneously biblical characters and contemporary people living in poverty. Many of the ideas and themes are borrowed from writers like Ched Myers and Bob Haverluck. The "resurrection" in this play takes place when Mary is lifted up from despair by the spirit of resistance and hope.

A Prairie Nativity was written for a barnyard Christmas service on the Circle Marsh pastoral charge in Plumas, Manitoba, in 1996. It takes the Christmas story and sets it in a modern Canadian prairie context, with the audience as a choir of angels in snowsuits and toques. (The temperature on the night of the first performance was minus 36! Thank goodness for the barn cats who tried to keep us warm.)

An early draft of *Maybe One?: A Theatrical History of the United Church* was written in 1990, and then extensively revised and updated for the 75th anniversary of the United Church of Canada, in 2000. It is by no means an authoritative history. It's just some events and issues I found interesting, translated into a series of sketches and pop-culture references.

Some helpful hints, & DOs and DON'Ts

Whether you're reading these plays, thinking about performing these or other plays, or creating your own plays:

DO let your audience use their imagination. It makes them more actively involved in the drama if they have to fill in gaps for themselves. In other words…

DON'T build extensive, complicated, realistic sets. It's too much hassle, and given the number of scenes in some of these plays, it's just not practical. The same goes for costumes. Try to focus on a few key "signifiers" that are essential for indicating a character (e.g. a crown for a king, a clerical collar or an alb for a minister, etc.). Remember, things like costumes and sets and props are just "stuff." The most important element in any drama is the interaction between characters.

DON'T try to find 63 actors for "Maybe One?" or 35 for "David's Rule." I mean, what are you – nuts?! Most of the longer plays in this collection were written for an ensemble cast of five to twelve actors, each of whom would play many different characters in the play. Someone playing a major character might only have one part, whereas another actor might play ten or twelve different minor characters. That way every gets a relatively equal time on stage.

DON'T assume that male characters can only be played by male actors, or female characters by female actors. Audiences are smart enough to know the difference between an actor and a character, as long as you give them clues and the parts are played with integrity. Occasionally a female actor will find something unexpected in a male character that a male actor might miss.

DO be creative about your use of space. In real life, people don't stand in rows. Use different areas of your playing space. Use different levels. (As long as it makes sense.) And for goodness sake…

DO move! Don't just stand there; keep the play active. (That's why they call it "acting.") But remember, moving is not the same as wandering. If you're going to move, move for a reason.

DO read the stage directions. I tend not to write things like, "So-and-so moves down-stage-left, checks the time of the gold-plated Victorian clock sitting on the mantle, before crossing upstage center to exit through the French doors." I'm more likely to say things like, "So-and-so enters," or "So-and-so leaves," and then leave it up to you to figure out where So-and-so is coming from or going to. (Or even *who* the heck is So-and-so?) As much as possible, I try to describe only those actions that are important to the story. So don't skip over them.

DO pay attention to ellipses. ("Ellipsis" is the word for those three dots you sometimes find in writing; as in, "It's a bird! It's a plane! It's… oh, it *is* a bird.) The ellipsis is one of my favorite bits of punctuation. At the end of a line it means someone has been cut off, or is just trailing off into silence. At the beginning of a line it means that the character is trying to think of what to say. In the middle of a line it usually means something unspoken is happening – the character is having a realization, or a moment of doubt, or just a thought. The ellipsis is usually as important or more important than the spoken line, so pay attention.

DO take your specific audience and playing space into consideration. If you're performing in a huge cathedral to an audience of older people with hearing aids, using microphones might be a good idea. In a smaller space it may not be as important.

DO get the rights to perform these plays. People in the church, I've found, tend to be very good about making sure that artists get compensated for their work. The easiest way to find out about royalties and permission to perform these plays is **to e-mail me at** scottdouglas.woodlake.com, let me know which play you want to perform, and I'll let you know what's involved.

DON'T think that the only plays you can perform are ones found in a book. In fact, I believe the best way to find a play that will be meaningful to your group or community is to create it yourself. Find the storytellers and dramatists in your own midst, and help them to create a play that speaks directly to your context. Playwriting is work, but it's not magic. Don't be afraid to give it a try.

STRANGE ANGELS

SCENE 1

[A bus stop on a city street. Nearby is a ladder from a construction site. Joe reads the newspaper as he waits for the bus.

Karl, a street person, approaches, mumbling to himself. Karl wears thrift store clothing soaked in cigarette smoke, dust, and alcohol. His nose is large and red, like a clown. Karl notices Joe and wanders toward him. He seems shy but friendly, and he speaks with a lisp.]

Karl: Uh, good morning, sir, I was wondering…

Joe: I'm sorry.

Karl: What?

Joe: I'm sorry. I don't have any change.

Karl: Oh…

[Karl digs in his pocket and pulls out a handful of change, which he places in Joe's hand.]

Karl: The bus drivers don't like it when you get on without any change.

Joe: Oh, uh, thanks… Oh, hang on, I *do* have some change after all.

[Joe gives the money back, then goes back to reading his paper. He notices Karl looking at him.]

Joe: Are you waiting for the bus too?

Karl: No.

Joe: Oh.

[Joe tries going back to the paper, but can't help noticing that Karl is still staring at him.]

Joe: Is there something I can do for you?

Karl: For me? No, thank you.

[Another pause. Finally…]

Joe: What?

Karl: Don't you want to know?

Joe: …Know what?

Karl: What the message is.

Joe: What message?

Karl: The message I have to give you.

Joe: I think maybe you've mistaken me for someone else.

Karl: No. The message is for you.

Joe: I'm sorry, I don't know you, and I'm not expecting a message.

    [Joe goes back to his paper.]

Karl: Oh… I understand. I see. I'm sorry.

Joe: That's OK.

Karl: I'm sorry. I didn't mean to…

Joe: Don't worry about it.

Karl: I should have introduced myself better. I'm an angel.

    [Joe looks at him warily.]

Joe: OK.

Karl: Do you believe me?

Joe: Not really.

Karl: I am.

Joe: OK.

Karl: Do you mean that?

Joe: Not really.

Karl: I have no reason to lie to you. Why don't you believe I'm an angel?

Joe: I don't know, I guess because I've never met an angel before.

Karl: My name's Karl.

Joe: Hi.

    [Joe goes back to his paper.]

Karl: So?

Joe: So…

Karl: Don't you want to know what the message is?

Joe: Uh… sure.

Karl: So you believe I'm an angel now.

     [Joe doesn't answer the question.]

Karl: It's the appearance, isn't it? You expect your angels to have long blonde hair and white gowns, or to look like popular movie actors… OK, look, I'll prove it. Here.

     [Karl pulls a piece of paper from his pocket and hands it to Joe.]

Joe: It's a Burger King napkin with the word "angel" written on it in blue felt marker.

Karl: Exactly. That proves I'm an angel. See? "Angel," right there.

Joe: In blue marker.

Karl: Yes.

Joe: On a Burger King napkin.

Karl: Yes.

Joe: OK.

Karl: It's all right to be scared.

Joe: I'm not scared.

Karl: 'Cause meeting an angel is a scary thing, so if you're scared, that's OK. I'm scared too, 'cause I know what they do to angels if they catch them… Are you a religious person?

Joe: Sorry?

Karl: Are you religious? Do you go to church, or synagogue, or temple…?

Joe: I go to church.

Karl: So you pray and stuff?

Joe: Uh, yeah.

Karl: How?

Joe: What do you mean?

Karl: How do you pray? What does it look like?

Joe: Head bowed, eyes closed. Pretty normal, I suppose.

[Karl bows his head stiffly and mumbles a monotone Lord's Prayer.]

Karl: OurFatherwhoartinheaven, hallowedbethyname, thykingdomcome, thywillbedone, onearthasitisinheaven...

Joe: Sure, maybe something like that.

Karl: Well, that explains it then. You're just timid. You want to know how angels pray?

[Before Joe can answer, Karl winds up his arms, then stands on one foot, reaches out wide, and speaks in a loud voice.]

Karl: OH!! Creator, you are the greatest thing since sliced bread! You are that orange powdery stuff in a box of Kraft Dinner! You are the public library on a cold, drizzly day. Oh, oh, oh, OH Creator, times are tough and we sure could use a helping hand, or at least a breather. And while you're at it, make this guy believe I'm an angel so I can deliver the message you asked me to deliver. Oh, oh, oh, oh, oh, oh, oh, oh O-klahoma!! Where the winds come sweeping down the plain, and the waving wheat can sure smell sweet when the wind comes right behind the rain! – just a little joke there – OK, um, don't let the bastards get you down. Angel Karl signing off. Over and out. Amen.

[Karl lowers his arms comes back down on both feet.]

Karl: That's how angels pray.

Joe: Hmm, interesting.

Karl: OK, OK, OK, look, how about this? If I'm not an angel, how do you explain the fact that I know everything about you? Like your name is Abraham McKenzie-Stewart, you were born in Musqudobit Harbor on the eighth of July, 1965. Your mother's name is Doris, your father's name is Lloyd, your wife's name is Cathy, your cat's name is William Lion Mackenzie King. You're an insurance broker, your favorite snack is peanut brittle, you like contemporary jazz, your eyes are brown, your shoes are size nine, your furniture is from IKEA, and you're taking the bus to work because your green Honda Accord is in the shop getting the transmission fixed... How about that?

Joe: That's amazing! That's absolutely incredible!... Not one right answer. Not even one! Not even the color of my eyes, and you can *see* that.

Karl: So I don't do party tricks. It doesn't mean I don't have a message for you.

Joe: Maybe you should just say what you have to say.

Karl: Do you believe I'm an angel?

Joe: No. No, I don't.

Karl: If you don't accept that I'm an angel then you won't accept the message and I'll have wasted a trip.

Joe: OK, well, whatever.

[Joe goes back to the paper. Karl stares at him. Joe realizes he isn't leaving.]

Joe: Look… Karl, is it?

Karl: Kar-ul.

Joe: Karl. Now I don't know what kind of a scam you're trying to pull, but…

Karl: Kar-ul.

Joe: …What did I say?

Karl: Karl.

Joe: And what is it supposed to be?

Karl: Kar-ul.

Joe: Karl.

Karl: Kar-ul.

Joe: Karl.

Karl: Kar-ul! It's an angel name. Like Mike-*ul*. Gabri-*ul*. Kar-*ul*.

Joe: Kar-*ul*.

Karl: Exactly!

Joe: Great. So, Kar-*ul*, it's been very interesting to talk to you, but my bus is coming soon, so… Goodbye.

Karl: [realizing] I know what the problem is.

[Karl runs backstage. Sounds of rummaging, clanging garbage can lids, rustling papers. Joe goes back to reading his paper.

MUSIC: *Ride of the Valkyries* by Wagner. Karl slowly and dramatically emerges wearing a pair of angel wings made of chicken wire and Styrofoam.]

Karl: Now do you believe me?

Joe: You have wings.

Karl: Yes!

Joe: They're very nice.

Karl: Thank you!

[Joe goes back to his paper.]

Karl: Oh, come on! Wait, wait…

[Karl climbs a nearby ladder, straddling the top like an angel on a Christmas tree.]

Karl: [singing] *O tannenbaum, O tannenbaum, wie treu sind deine Blätter*… It's like a Christmas tree, and I'm the angel…

Joe: I'm going down to the next bus stop now, OK?

Karl: But what about the message? I'm supposed to give you a message.

Joe: I guess you'll have to give it to somebody else.

Karl: But it's not for somebody else, it's for you.

Joe: No it's not for me, Karl! I'm just some guy you found at a bus stop who was polite enough to tolerate your ramblings for a little while. But now I'd like to be left alone, all right? You're a complete stranger.

[Joe starts to walk away. Karl watches him leave, and, to his own surprise, suddenly "knows" something.]

Karl: Your name is Joe. You live in a two-bedroom apartment by yourself. You leave the TV on, even when you're not watching, because the silence makes you nervous. You're not sure you like this city. You've lived here three years and you still don't have any close friends. You hate bars, you don't know the names of the people who live around you, and your family lives in another province. You feel disconnected. No… *Lonely*.

[Joe stops in his tracks. He turns and walks back to Karl. Karl takes a step back, in case Joe tries to slug him.]

Joe: What's the message?

Karl: That's it, isn't it? You're lonely.

Joe: …Yes.

Karl: So you want to know the message?

Joe: I do.

Karl: And you believe that I'm an angel?

Joe: I think I do. Is that nuts?

Karl: Sure. Come here, I'll give you the message.

[Joe moves toward him. Karl motions him closer, as if about to tell him a secret. Joe steps closer. Karl reaches out and thumps him on the forehead.]

Karl: My work here is done.

[Karl turns and leaves. Joe stands stunned for a moment, then wanders off, confused.]

SCENE 2

[A symposium on angels. Marsha enters, wearing silk scarves and crystals – very New Age.]

Marsha: Angels take many forms, though they do not have material bodies like you or me. They are beings of pure light, harmonic crystallizations of the universe's positive energy. Angels are expressions of God's unconditional love and they want only good for us.

I'd like to tell you about my first encounter with my guardian angel – Oprael. It was about five years ago. I was sitting at home, watching *The Nature of Things*, when suddenly, out of the blue, David Suzuki tells me that the earth will be unlivable within 20 years. And BANG, I go into a panic attack! I'm crying, I'm screaming, I'm trying to climb under the couch, because suddenly I imagine myself as an ancient fossil on a barren and lifeless planet spinning through empty space and there's nothing I can do about it! I am freaking out! I'm downing valium like Tic-Tacs, just trying to keep from pulling the curtains off the wall. And then suddenly… Suddenly, I am bathed in a warm glow. A golden light flows over me like honey. And standing there, beside the TV, is the most beautiful…person, being, creature, angel. And she says to me, "Marsha, be thou not afraid. All shalt be well." …And I knew it was true. I knew that everything would be all right, that the angels were in control, and I didn't need to be worried anymore. So I shut off the TV, I shut off David Suzuki, I stopped worrying about the environment, and since that time I have been nothing but happy, serene, and personally fulfilled.

[Marsha floats off.]

SCENE 3

[The city again. Joe enters, looking for Karl. He checks up and down streets. Finally he finds Karl in a corner.]

Joe: There you are!!

[Karl instinctively bolts. Joe runs after him.]

Joe: Wait! Come back!

Karl: I didn't do it! It wasn't me.

Joe: Wait!

> [Joe catches him. Karl quickly takes off his shoes and hands them to Joe.]

Karl: I didn't know they were yours, honest! I was just borrowing them; I was going to bring them back.

Joe: I don't want the shoes.

Karl: Well, I can't give you any money for them.

Joe: They're not my shoes. I'm Joe. You delivered a message to me this morning?

> [Karl looks very, very closely at him, then recognizes him.]

Karl: Oh, you, yeah! How's that going?

> [Karl puts the shoes back on, sitting to tie the laces.]

Joe: I've spent the whole day looking for you. I was starting to think you'd… you know, back to heaven.

Karl: Oh no, no. First I got to deliver the message, then I got to wait for it to take. That's the hard part there, waiting for it to take.

Joe: You know, you were right; it *was* the appearance thing. All I saw was a crazy street person who was likely trying to con me. I didn't know that angels travel in disguise.

Karl: Well, that's what the wings are for.

Joe: What?

Karl: To travel in "de skies."

Joe: Angel joke?

Karl: Angel joke.

Joe: Nice. Look, I'm glad I found you, because ever since this morning I've been… I've been trying to… You know… OK, here's the thing – I don't get it.

Karl: Don't get what?

Joe: The message. I don't get it. I don't know what it means.

Karl: I could repeat it for you.

Joe: No! No, I remember it, I just don't… understand.

Karl: Geez, that's rough.

Joe: So… what does it mean?

[Karl shrugs and starts to leave.]

Joe: No, wait, you've got to explain it. It's been bugging me all day.

Karl: I'm sorry, I just deliver the messages, I don't interpret them. You maybe want a theologian or something.

Joe: You must have *some* idea what it means. Does it have to do with my job?

Karl: I don't think so… Maybe it means you have a bug on your forehead.

Joe: Why would God send a message that I have a bug on my forehead?

Karl: If it was a big bug.

Joe: It's not about a bug! Now come on, just give me a clue.

Karl: I'm sorry, Joe. At best I'd be making an educated guess.

Joe: That's all I'm looking for.

[Pause.]

Karl: I think it means you're going to die.

[Joe goes pale.]

Karl: I'm sorry I had to be the one to break it to you.

Joe: I'm going to die.

Karl: I'm afraid so.

Joe: But how? When?

Karl: Couldn't tell you.

Joe: But soon, though.

Karl: Maybe.

Joe: …Maybe?

Karl: Maybe soon. Maybe not soon. Maybe in a hundred years. Hard to say.

Joe: Let me get this straight, when you say I'm going to die, you mean *someday*.

Karl: Yes.

Joe: *Someday* I'm going to die.

Karl: Yes.

Joe: You're an angel, you've been sent to earth to deliver a message, and that message is that someday, eventually, I'm going to die.

Karl: I understand that it must come as quite a shock to you.

Joe: Karl, I know that I'm going to die.

Karl: I don't think so.

Joe: Yes, yes, I do.

Karl: No, no, you don't. I know how you live. You don't live like someone who knows he's going to die. You live like someone expecting to live forever and planning to sleepwalk through the next thousand years. You're on automatic pilot, Joe, and someday you're going to wake up and say, "Oop, I'm dead." I think that's what *this* means, Joe…

[He thumps Joe on the forehead again.]

Karl: It means "Wake up." Wake up and pay attention to what's going on around you. There are wonderful things going on all around you. Sure, there's terrible things too, but that's all part of the Mystery, Joe. The real world is marvelous and strange. How many strangers do you meet in a day?

Joe: I take the bus every morning.

Karl: But do you *meet* those people, Joe? Do you actually get to know them? Or are they just background noise? You've got to meet more strangers, Joe. And what's more, you've got to let them be strange. This isn't just a place to catch the bus on the way to somewhere else. This is your life. You've got to pay attention, stop, and listen for a second. Just listen. What do you hear?

Joe: Nothing.

Karl: That's because you're not listening, Joe. Now listen. What do you hear?

Joe: Cars, trucks…

Karl: The kids playing in the schoolyard?

Joe: Yeah.

Karl: The two Laotian men at the corner store discussing the price of apples?

Joe: No.

Karl: Listen carefully.

Joe: OK, I've got it now. How do you know they're...

Karl: How about smells. What do you smell?

Joe: Someone needs a bath.

Karl: That's probably me. What else?

Joe: Someone's cooking with curry.

Karl: Yeah.

Joe: Someone's smoking tobacco.

Karl: And do you feel the earth under your feet?

Joe: Yes.

Karl: And do you see the *taraxucum officinale* pushing through the cracks in the sidewalk?

Joe: The what?

Karl: The weed.

Joe: Oh, yeah.

Karl: Pay attention to that weed, Joe. God likes that weed. Maybe that's why it grows so well. People, on the other hand, pull up weeds every chance they get. They devote whole fields to one single crop. And you know what happens then.

Joe: No, what?

Karl: The crop doesn't encounter any strangers, it never has to adapt, it stops evolving, and then one day a crop disease comes along and wipes out the whole species. That's what happens when you impose a monoculture on an ecosystem at the expense of biodiversity. You open up the door to widespread systematic extinction.

Joe: I think I understand what you're talking about... You sure know a lot about plants.

Karl: Masters degree in biology... What?

Joe: I don't know what surprises me more – a street person with a masters degree or an angel with a masters degree.

Karl: It was a long time ago.

Joe: How long?

Karl: Mid-80s.

Joe: That *is* a long time ago.

Karl: I was married back then, but it didn't work out.

Joe: You know, that's a bit more history than I look for in an angel.

Karl: I had a little girl, too. Four years old. At least, she was four when the troubles started.

Joe: The troubles?

Karl: The troubles in my head. With the doctors.

Joe: Did the doctors have a name for these troubles?

Karl: Most probably some form of schizophrenia, but, you know, mental illness is a tricky thing and it's hard to be certain.

> [Joe gets up and moves away from Karl.]

Karl: What's the matter?

Joe: This whole angel thing is just a fantasy, isn't it.

Karl: Oh yeah, sure, absolutely, I mean, no doubt about it. Delusions are part of the condition. But the thing is – and I could never get the doctors to understand this – I'm not a mentally ill guy who thinks he's an angel; I'm a mentally ill *angel*, who thinks he's an angel. That's a big difference, don't you think?

> [Karl notices Joe moving away.]

Karl: Joe?

> [Joe tries to appear helpful, while still keeping his distance.]

Joe: Look, is there some place that you need to go? Somebody I should contact? Maybe I could get you to a doctor, prescribe some medication…?

Karl: [disappointed] Don't do this, Joe!

Joe: Maybe an emergency room…

> [Karl freaks out in agitated frustration.]

Karl: Don't do this!! This, this, this *thing* you do. I can see you doing it! You've finally found a category to put me in, a slot that makes sense! You've stripped away all my *strangeness* and, and, and, and you're placing me in a file that only asks for pity and guilt. I don't want to be in that file, Joe! My wings alone are too big for that file!

[Joe is stunned by this outburst.]

Joe: OK, whatever. I was just trying to help. But if you don't want my help, that's fine…

[Joe starts to walk away. Karl stands and yells after him.]

Karl: You want to know why you're so lonely, Joe? You want to know why you feel disconnected? It's because you *are* disconnected! The only people you know are the ones you create in your head! You reduce every person you meet to a category, you define them, you classify them. That way you don't have to deal with their ambiguities. That way you can live in your own little movie theater, where everything is safe and sterile, and you never have to be confused, or feel awkward, or, God forbid, *learn* anything!!

[Joe stops.]

Karl: You spent the whole day looking for an angel because you wanted to know what the message meant. You thought it might be important, it might have to do with salvation. But when you finally found the angel you got scared. So you found an excuse to ignore him. If that's what you want to do, fine! But the message stands. I'm not just the messenger, Joe, I'm the message. You hear that, Joe? I'm the message.

[Joe returns. Pause.]

Joe: So, what now?

Karl: Do you believe I'm an angel?

Joe: Yes, I believe you're an angel.

Karl: You're just saying that because I made you feel guilty.

Joe: I believe you're an angel, all right!

[Karl smiles.]

Karl: All right.

[Karl starts to climb the ladder.]

Joe: What are you doing, Karl?

Karl: I'm going to fly, Joe. You believe I can fly, don't you?

Joe: Yes, I believe you can fly, but…

Karl: You have faith, don't you?

Joe: Yes, but…

Karl: Well then?

Joe: I'm just thinking now may not be the best time to demonstrate.

Karl: No time like the present, Joe.

Joe: Karl, come on down.

Karl: You've got to believe, Joe. If you believe, then I can fly.

Joe: Oh, don't say that, Karl. I'm still getting over the time Tinkerbell died because I didn't clap my hands hard enough.

Karl: Clear the runway, Joe. I'm ready to jump…

Joe: Karl, stop!

Karl: Slip the surly bonds of earth and all that…

Joe: Karl!

Karl: Prepare to be awestruck.

> [Karl jumps out into the air… and plummets straight to the ground, landing in a clanking, clattering pile.]

Joe: Karl!!

> [Joe rushes over to Karl and drags him to a flat piece of ground. Karl is a crumpled mass.]

Karl: Ooohhhh…

Joe: Are you all right? Can you move?

Karl: I think my back is broken.

Joe: Oh my God, I shouldn't have moved you.

> [Joe starts to drag Karl back to where he landed.]

Karl: [urgently] Don't put me back! Don't put me back!

Joe: OK, Karl, you're going to be fine. I'm going to go call an ambulance.

Karl: No time! Damage too severe! Spine shattered. Internal organs crushed. Only thing that will save me now… is a miracle.

Joe: A miracle.

Karl: You've got to pray, Joe. Pray for a miracle.

[Joe sighs, then bows his head.]

Joe: [perfunctory] God, please help Karl…

Karl: No, Joe. You've got to pray the way the angels pray.

[Joe looks at Karl doubtfully. He rolls his eyes, takes a deep breath, sticks his arms out, stands on one foot, and prays.]

Joe: Oh Creator, you are the greatest thing since sliced bread. You are that…

Karl: Orange powdery stuff.

Joe: Orange powdery stuff in a box of Kraft Dinner… This is really embarrassing, you know.

Karl: You're doing fine.

Joe: You are the…

Karl: Public library.

Joe: …Public library on a cold, drizzly day. Oh, oh, oh Creator, your angel Karl here has apparently broken every bone in his body and he needs a miracle to heal him. Make him whole so he can continue doing your work. Oh, oh, oh, O-klahoma!! Where the winds come sweeping down the plain, etc, etc. …Much appreciated. Joe signing off. Over and out. Amen.

Karl: Joe, it's working!

Joe: [not too surprised] Really.

Karl: I can feel it. I'm healing.

[Karl bursts up onto his feet.]

Karl: You did it, Joe!

[Karl rambunctiously kisses Joe.]

Joe: You're really strange, you know that, Karl.

Karl: There's a woman at a bus stop on Broadway, and we have to deliver a message. Come on, let's fly.

[As Karl starts on his way, he trips and falls. He jumps back up.]

Karl: I'm OK, I'm OK!

[Karl rushes off. Joe watches him go and considers sneaking off in the opposite direction, but finally decides to follow. The end. MUSIC: *Oklahoma* by Rodgers and Hammerstein.]

DOG EAT DOG WORLD

[Two dogs and a cat. One dog, Rufus, wears a worn sweatshirt and jeans. The other dog, Fido, wears a suit and reads a newspaper. The cat, Rev. Whiskers, wears a clerical collar. Rufus addresses the audience.]

Rufus: [to audience] Hi, there. My name's Rufus. I'm a hound-dog. I guess I've kinda always been a hound-dog. My parents were hound-dogs. And most likely my kids'll grow up to be hound-dogs. I mean, I'd *like* to be one of those classy show-type dogs, but I can't really see it happening. So mostly I just try to be the best hound-dog I can be... It ain't easy sometimes. I don't have much in the way of money. I live below the poverty line, so I guess I'm what you'd call a poor dog. I have to rely on welfare to get by. If there was some other way I could survive I would, 'cause I find going down to the welfare office kinda demeaning. They make you sit. They make you beg. They make you jump through hoops. And finally, if they decide you're needy enough, they throw you a bone. A small bone. It usually isn't enough to get me through the month. Rev. Whiskers, do you have any words of comfort for someone like me?

Rev. Whiskers: Meow, Rufus. On behalf of the church, I'd like to say, Blessed are the poor... um, in spirit. For theirs is the kingdom of heaven... Which, um, doesn't do them a lot of good *now*, but, well, you know...

Fido: Whine, whine, whine! My name is Fido. It's a Latin name; it means "faithful." And I like to think that I am. I attend church regularly, and, when I go away on vacation, I leave postdated checks to keep up my contributions. I'm a good dog. Yes I am. Yes I am. But what I'm reading in this newspaper has me barking mad. Apparently, the reason that my taxes are so high is because of all the money the government spends on welfare and social programs.

Rev. Whiskers: Actually, Fido, the government spends more on tax breaks to businesses and investors.

Fido: But those are investments that stand to benefit regular Canadians like me; they're not a drain on the government coffers that only benefit the poor.

Rufus: I'm sorry, did you just say that poor people aren't regular Canadians?

Fido: Don't get me wrong. I have nothing against welfare. I think it's great to help out those who really *need* help – you know, strays with broken legs and nobody to look after them – that sort of thing. But there are lots of dogs who apply for welfare just because they're too lazy to work. And, apparently, welfare fraud is a big problem. I saw it on a billboard. That's why the economy is going to the dogs. And that's why I have to pay such a big part of my hard-earned income, providing perks for the poor and unemployed.

[Fido rolls up the newspaper and smacks Rufus on the nose.]

Rufus: Hey!

Fido: When I was a young pup I learned the value of money. I learned to budget, to make every dollar count. But these welfare recipients… No sooner do they get their checks than they've got them cashed and they're spending their money on junk food and booze and VLTs. It's like you set out the bowl of dog food and say, "This has got to last you all week." And 20 minutes later they've gobbled it all up and they're lying on the floor bloated and sick.

Rufus: Do you *know* any welfare recipients?

[Fido smacks him.]

Rufus: OW!!

Fido: There's got to be a way to make sure that people use their money for what it's supposed to be used for, instead of squandering it all on luxuries. They should be paying rent, buying food, proper clothes for their kids, stuff like that. Not putting down two payments on a powerboat and then having it repossessed. Not buying golf clubs or CDs or fancy sneakers.

Rev. Whiskers: By the way, Fido, do you have anything to donate to the church's garage sale?

Fido: Oh sure, I've got a load of crap in the basement. I'll drop it by next week… But my point is, we've got to keep these welfare recipients on a short leash. That's the only way they'll learn to look after themselves.

[Fido smacks Rufus.]

Rufus: OK, I'm asking you to stop!

Fido: If you want my opinion, if people want money they should work for it. Even if it's just sweeping the street, scooping up poop, whatever. It's the symbolism of the thing. Nobody wants a handout. They want to *earn* their money. That way, you don't get paid unless you deserve it.

Rufus: How much money do you make a year?

Fido: That's none of your business!

Rufus: The money that you make, do you *deserve* it?

Fido: Of course I deserve it! I get up early in the morning. I work like a dog all day. I make phone calls, I go to meetings. Sometimes I even work through my lunch break. I earn every penny through hard work and dogged determination.

Rufus: But I work hard too. I know lots of people who work hard. I'm talking *hard labor*, sometimes at tedious and demeaning jobs. And they don't get paid anywhere near as much as you. So why do you deserve to have more money?

Fido: OK, granted. It's not fair. It's a dog's life. I'm better off than a lot of people and that's just my good luck. God has blessed me with a good job, a nice house, and a loving family. And all I can do is look at those less fortunate and say, "There but for the grace of God go I."

Rufus: So your wealth is a blessing from God.

Fido: The little wealth that I have – I'm not a rich dog. But yes, I feel blessed by God.

Rufus: So where does that leave the poor? Where does that leave me? Is my poverty a sign that I'm *cursed* by God?

Fido: Uh, Rev. Whiskers?

Rev. Whiskers: Oh, gosh, that's a dicey theological question, isn't it? There's quite a spectrum of opinions on that subject…

Fido: Poverty is a sin. You said that in a sermon.

[Fido smacks Rufus.]

Rev. Whiskers: I did? Oh, yes, I did. But I was talking in terms of corporate, systemic sin…

Rufus: Poverty is a sin, but being poor isn't. It's not my fault that I'm poor, I don't choose to be poor, and stop smacking me on the nose!!

[Fido smacks Rufus.]

Fido: Stop your barking!

Rufus: Stop smacking me on the nose!

[Fido smacks Rufus.]

Rufus: I told you to stop!

[Fido smacks Rufus. Rufus growls menacingly at Fido.]

Fido: I knew it. You've got to watch this breed. They'll turn on you.

Rufus: All right, I'm tired of this.

Fido: Yikes! Stay back! Staaay, staaay. Don't you bare your teeth at me, you mongrel.

Rufus: Look, Fido…

Fido: That's *Mr.* Fido to you.

Rufus: Why do you keep hitting me?!?

Fido: What do you mean, why do I keeping hitting you?

Rufus: You keep hitting me on the nose! Why?

Fido: You're a dog.

Rufus: You're a dog too!

Fido: There's no need to be insulting.

Rufus: I'm not being insulting! You're a dog! We're both dogs! That's the premise of this play: "What if people were dogs." Get it? We're *all* dogs!

Rev. Whiskers: I'm not. I'm a cat.

Rufus: Well, of course *you're* a cat. You represent the church, so you spend much of your time sitting on the fence.

Rev. Whiskers: I think that's a bit unfair. I'm just trying to uphold my justice-seeking integrity while trying to be sensitive to Fido, who happens to be an influential member of my congregation…

Rufus: And while you're pussyfooting around, he's smacking me on the nose.

Fido: Look, I don't see what the problem is.

Rufus: The problem is, you're a dog, and I'm a dog, but you seem to think it's all right to roll up a newspaper and smack me on the nose with it. You talk about me as if I'm part of some other species. You act as if you have the right to *train* me, or something. I don't mind being treated like a dog, but being treated like a dog *by* a dog…!

Fido: All right, I'm sorry if I've offended you in any way. But it's nothing personal. I wasn't talking about you; I was talking about the poor *in general*.

Rufus: There are no poor "in general." There are real dogs with real lives.

Fido: I don't expect you to agree with my opinion, but I have a right to say what I think.

Rufus: My problem isn't with what you *think*, Fido. It's what you *say*. It's what you *do*. Your comments make others think less of those of us who live in poverty. They make those of us living in poverty think less of ourselves. We've got enough self-esteem problems to deal with without you tearing us down.

Fido: Don't forget, I'm a good dog. I'm a very, very good dog. I go to church; I've read the Bible. I love my neighbors. On both sides! I even like the folks *two* houses down.

Rev. Whiskers: Rufus, you're right. I *have* been sitting on the fence. It's time for me to take action. Our God has a preferential option for the poor, and it's time that I did too. I'm going to commit myself to making change in this society. I'm going to work at ending poverty and protesting the systems that oppress the poor. I'm going to take a leap of faith, and, God willing, I'll land on my feet. Starting now! [Long pause.] I'm bored of that. I'm going to go look for something to eat.

[Rev. Whiskers leaves.]

Fido: I hear what you're saying, but you can't teach an old dog new tricks.

Rufus: But who taught you those tricks in the first place?

Fido: What do you mean?

Rufus: I mean, where did you get the idea that welfare recipients always squander their money?

Fido: I don't know. I read it somewhere.

Rufus: And who told you that the poor are responsible for the national debt and your high taxes?

Fido: I heard it from some politician. You know, that one on TV.

Rufus: And where did you learn that you can *earn* your keep, and survival should be dependent on working?

Fido: I don't know, it's just what I think.

Rufus: Turn around and find out who's yanking your choke chain, Fido. Who stands to benefit from you blaming the poor for the problems in the economy? Who benefits from your being afraid of me, and your working hard not to become like me? Who benefits from your looking down on me instead of looking up?

Fido: Wait a minute. Are you saying that I've been *trained*? That somebody rings a bell and I salivate? That's preposterous.

Rufus: Is it? Think about it.

[Fido tilts his head to one side and then the other.]

Fido: Hmm, now that you mention it, I remember this yummy-looking biscuit from when I was a pup. It was always being held just in front of my nose, and there was a voice saying…

[A human being with a large rolled up newspaper enters and smacks Fido on the nose. Fido yelps.]

Human: Bad dog! Don't bite the hand that feeds you! Bad! Now go and lie down.

[The human being leaves. Fido looks after the human. Fido looks at Rufus. Fido looks after the human. He's shakes his head, confused.]

Fido: [to Rufus] Now look what you did!

[Fido smacks Rufus.]

Rufus: What *I* did?!

Fido: Why do dogs like you always have to raise a racket? Yelping and whining and barking. You all ought to be shipped off to the pound.

Rufus: The pound. That's always the answer, isn't it? If nobody wants them, ship them off to the pound. Lock them up. Put them to sleep. Well, you know what, Fido? You're the one who's asleep. And if you say that the poor are to blame, if you say the poor are poor because they're lazy, or they're stupid, if you say that the poor are all violent criminals and cheaters and thieves, if that's what you say, then, buddy, you're *lying*. And I'm not content to let sleeping dogs lie.

Fido: You're just mad because I won't bite the hand that feeds me. I'm a good dog. I'm not a bad dog, I'm a good dog. And I shouldn't have to be supporting you. There should be organizations whose job it is to look after the poor, so I don't have to. The S.P.C.A, or the Humane Society, or something.

Rufus: Face it, Fido, if this was a humane society, I wouldn't *be* poor.

[Rufus leaves. Fido leaves. The end.]

A FAIR TRADE

(For use with Matthew 20:1–16)

[A man and a woman sit at a typical Canadian breakfast table, drinking coffee. Mildred – in her 50s or 60s, and a little bit clueless – is wearing a dressing gown and slippers. The man's face is hidden behind the newspaper he is reading.]

Mildred: I hope the coffee's not too strong for you this morning, dear. The coffeemaker's been acting up again. Of course, some people like strong coffee. Do you remember that restaurant where they sell the ridiculously overpriced coffee? What was the name of that restaurant again? Oh well, I don't suppose it matters…

[Mildred ad-libs more morning chit-chat, perhaps including references to events or people known to the audience. The man behind the newspaper never responds. Finally…]

Mildred: Walter… Walter! Are you listening to me?

[The man lowers the newspaper to reveal Jesus Morales (pronounced *hey-zoos mo-rah-lays*), a Nicaraguan coffee farmer. He wears work clothes, bare feet, and a cap or straw hat. He smiles.]

Jesus: *Buenos días, señora.*

Mildred: Waah!! You're not Walter. Where's Walter? Where's my husband? Who are you? How did you get here? What are you doing in my kitchen?

Jesus: I have come about your coffee, señora.

Mildred: My coffee…? Oh, I get it! You're Juan Valdez!

Jesus: No, señora, my name is Jesus Morales…

Mildred: I've seen all your commercials. Where's your mule?

Jesus: I'm not Juan Valdez! My name is Jesus Morales.

Mildred: Are you related to Juan?

Jesus: Distant cousin. I am a *cafetelero*, a coffee farmer, from Nicaragua. I have come to you because I've heard that you are a Christian woman and that you wish to do good in the world.

Mildred: Well, yes, hubby and I go to church regularly and try to give to charities and such, but…

Jesus: Then it is very important that you know where your coffee comes from.

Mildred: I know where my coffee comes from – Safeway, aisle seven. What I want to know is, where has my husband gone?

Jesus: Your husband and I have magically exchanged places. Call it a "fair trade" if you like. I am at your breakfast table and he is on my coffee farm in Nicaragua.

[A befuddled Walter, still wearing pajamas, enters a different part of the playing space. He looks around, confused.]

Walter: Mildred? Mildred, where are you? Have you turned the thermostat up?

Jesus: Señora, may I tell you a story? It's sort of a parable, like the parable of the workers in the vineyard from the Bible… only completely different. Once upon a time there was a poor *cafetelero* who had a small three-hectare coffee farm in Nicaragua. (That would be me.)

[A group of five or six workers, dressed in work clothes, enter and gather around Walter. They welcome him with handshakes, slaps on the back, and calls of *"Bienvenido."* As Jesus tells the story, the workers encourage Walter to help them act it out in movement and mime. NOTE: Play this all for comedy. Poor Walter doesn't know what he's supposed to be doing or why. He can ad-lib reactions and commentary throughout, like "Gosh, this is hard work," or "How long until quitting time?" The Workers can have fun getting him to do the work. Walter is always a little behind, trying to catch up.]

Jesus: For three years we've been waiting for the coffee plants to produce fruit. It was hard to survive for those first three years, but finally there are ripe cherries on the branches, and it is time for the harvest. So we climb up the hill to the coffee plants (which grow only at certain heights) and we pick.

[The workers sling cloth pouches over their shoulders, give one to Walter, and then they climb the hill. Climb, climb, climb. And then they pick cherries from the coffee plant at shoulder height or higher. Pick, pick, pick. Jesus waits for them to complete the actions before continuing.]

Jesus: If a rain comes before we have finished picking, the cherries will be washed away, so we must pick quickly. When the pouches are full we take them down the hill where they can be fermented. We then separate the pulp from the bean. The pulp is returned to the soil as compost, while the beans are each washed by hand. It is a very laborious process.

[Descend, descend, descend. Dump cherries. Wait. Remove cherries. Grind, grind, grind. Throw compost. Scrub beans. Scrub, scrub, scrub.]

Jesus: Now we lay the beans out to dry. If there is a chance of rain, they must all be gathered up and taken inside.

[Spread out beans. One of the workers holds out a hand and checks for rain. She whistles to others, who quickly gather the beans. She whistles again, indicating false alarm, and the beans are spread out again. Walter and the workers are exhausted.]

Jesus: After two or three days the beans are dry. They can be put in sacks and taken to the cooperative warehouse.

[The workers load a huge sack of beans on Walter's back. They point down the aisle and give him directions.]

Walter: What? Where? How far? Two days!?! On foot!?! You've got to be kidding.

[The workers wave goodbye and exit. Walter carries the heavy sack down the aisle to the back of the audience.]

Jesus: You see, although we work very hard, we are very poor. There is no electricity where I live. No telephone, no medical facilities.

Mildred: Oh dear, I hope Walter remembered to take his pills. Tell me, Mr. Morales, if coffee doesn't pay very well, why don't you just do something else?

Jesus: We do not have the same opportunities that you do, señora. My country has received aid money from richer countries, and in order to pay back our debts we must devote much of our land to cash crops, like coffee, which will be sold back to those same rich countries.

[Mildred is about to take a sip of coffee, but stops and pushes the cup away from herself.]

Jesus: Things used to be worse. There was a time when we could only trade with a few powerful *comerciantes*, intermediaries, who only wanted money for themselves and cared nothing for us. Now we have a coffee farmer's cooperative and things are a little better. Someday our co-op may have enough money to provide a health clinic or a pharmacy for its members.

[One of the workers enters, wearing a jacket or a different hat to indicate that she is now a co-op worker. Walter comes back up the aisle, straining under the sack of beans. The co-op worker smiles and waves as Walter approaches.]

Co-op Worker: Good news, friend! Coffee went up three cents on the New York Exchange this morning.

Jesus: From the warehouse, all the sacks of coffee beans are taken by truck to the port.

[Co-op Worker and Walter get in a truck. Walter holds the sack on his lap. Drive, drive, drive, jostle, bump, swerve, screech. Four more workers enter and stand spread out in a line. The one farthest from Walter wears a suit jacket and holds a cup, indicating that he is a Consumer; the next one holds a coffee pot (Retailer); the next one wears a white coat (Roaster). The one closest to Walter wears a captain's cap (Shipper). The Shipper takes the sack and pretends to sort through the beans, throwing out the small ones.]

Jesus: At the port the beans are sifted by size. Only the largest can be exported. We would have more large beans if we used chemicals like other coffee farmers, but the chemicals are unhealthy and harmful to the environment. Once the beans are sifted and put in containers, they are loaded in ships and taken to North America, where they are roasted, ground, packaged, and shipped to the retailers.

> [The Shipper carries the sack to the Roaster. The Roaster turns his back, makes hissing and grinding sounds, and then turns back around holding a package of coffee.]

Mildred: Is roasting a difficult process?

Jesus: You could do it in about 20 minutes in your own oven.

> [The Roaster hands the package to the Retailer, who puts it in the pot and turns to the Consumer. He pours into the Consumer's cup.]

Retailer: Warm up your cup, sir?

Consumer: Thank you.

Mildred: How much is a sack of coffee worth?

Jesus: It depends on the year. Sometimes very little, sometimes very much. Let us say that today a sack might cost $1000.

> [The Consumer takes out a wad of bills and hands it to the Retailer. The Retailer takes out a chunk and passes it down the line. Each person takes a percentage of the cash.]

Jesus: But remember that 25% of the money you pay for coffee goes to the retailer. And more than half goes to the big companies that roast and grind and package and market. So by the time the *cafetelero* gets paid…

> [The stack of money finally gets to Walter, but it is much smaller. He counts the few bills in shock.]

Walter: Seventy dollars!?! For a $1000 sack? After I climbed and picked and de-pulped and washed and dried and carried all those beans?!

> [The Shipper, Roaster, and Retailer exit. The Co-op Worker gives him a sympathetic look and exits as well. The Consumer puts his arm around Walter's shoulder.]

Consumer: Look at it this way, Sancho. If you were making a decent living growing coffee, then everyone would want to do it. And then there'd be a glut on the coffee market and prices would drop to next to nothing. And you wouldn't want that, would you. So cheer up, and remember – your exploitation helps millions of North Americans start the day chipper and alert.

[The Consumer leaves. Walter looks at his little money, depressed.]

Jesus: And then there's the workers to pay.

[The workers joyously return, gather around Walter, take some money, thank Walter, and exit, leaving Walter with only one or two bills. Walter sits, defeated.]

Mildred: So the roasters and the retailers, who come late in the process and do little work of their own, receive the most reward. That's like the vineyard parable.

Jesus: Except that the vineyard parable is about God's generosity, and this story is about an unjust system that keeps me and my family poor.

Mildred: [taking a sip of coffee] Oh dear. This coffee tastes bitter now. Tell me, Mr. Morales, do I have to stop drinking coffee?

Jesus: There is a way that you can have fine-quality coffee and I can be fairly paid for my work. It's called the *comercio alternativo*, or Fair Trade. The Transfair logo on your coffee indicates that the company works in cooperation with *cafeteleros* like me, guaranteeing a minimum price that is fair and helping to improve social conditions in our communities. In return, we take extra care with the beans for the *comercio alternativo*. We send them our finest quality, organically grown beans, because they are in solidarity with us. Many churches invest in Fair Trade, because it is a practical way of doing justice in the world. Fair Trade is good for everyone.

Mildred: Thank you for coming, Mr. Morales. I was a bit disappointed at first, especially when I found out you were neither Juan Valdez nor Julio Iglesias, but I've learned a lot from your visit. You certainly have opened my eyes. Thank you.

[Pause. Jesus makes no move to leave.]

Mildred: Was there something else?

[Jesus points to her cup of coffee.]

Mildred: Oh! Oh. Well, you see, I'd really very much like to buy fairly traded coffee, but, you know how it is, creatures of habit, hubby is attached to the familiar taste of our regular brand...

Jesus: That's fine. I'll just make myself comfortable until you change your mind.

Mildred: Pardon my asking, but how long were you thinking of staying?

Jesus: Have you heard the expression, "The poor you shall have with you always"?

Mildred: Always...? Well, I suppose maybe it is time for a change. What did you say that symbol I should look for was called? Transfair?

Jesus: Señora, you are a good woman and I have enjoyed our breakfast together, but I must get back to the harvest. Señor?

[Walter looks up.]

Jesus: Fair trade?

Walter: Fair trade.

[Jesus and Walter shake hands and switch positions. Jesus exits. Walter kisses Mildred on the cheek, takes a swig of coffee, spits it out, and staggers off, exhausted.]

Walter: I'm going back to bed.

Mildred: Well, isn't that typical. Here I am raising my consciousness of global economics, and he just wants to sleep in.

[Walter and Mildred exit. The end.]

DAVID'S RULE

SCENE 1: THE GIANT SLAYER

[David plays guitar as the cast enters and sets up the playing area. They place their props: sticks, bowls, cloaks. These simple objects will be used to represent the various items in the story: swords, spears, etc. They set a ladder in the middle of the space. Then they move off to the sides as the Storyteller speaks to the audience. As she speaks she moves around the playing area, picking up a stick and putting it down, leaning on the ladder, trying on a cloak, etc. The other actors sit off to the side or at the back of the playing space, waiting to take up a character and enter.]

Storyteller: What is a story? Is a story a lie, a game of make-believe? Is a story the truth, a word written in stone? Is it simply getting from point A to point B? Or maybe it's rising action, climax, falling action, conclusion. What are the stories you were taught and carry with you? And what are the stories you will teach your children? Are your stories a cloak to keep you warm and safe? Or are they a cage, to hold you in place and keep others in line? Or are your stories a clay bowl, an open vessel for many dreams…? This is a story about David, who was a hero and a rogue, a trickster and a king, a rule-maker and a rule-breaker. If you want different words for this story, you can find them in a book called "Samuel," but for now this story is ours. So, our story needs a hero.

[David enters.]

Storyteller: This is David, a young boy, a shepherd. And for now I will be his little sister, Hannah, or Han. You'll need to use your imaginations to create the setting. Make it in your mind, for what you make in your mind is only a step away from real… So, let this ladder be a tree, nice for shade and good for climbing. Around the tree make a lush green field, and people it with sheep.

All: Baaah, baaaah.

Storyteller/Han: Excellent. If you can imagine a field and a tree and a boy and his sister playing tag, then you've made space for the story and we can begin. So, on your mark, get set, go.

[David and Han play tag. David touches the ladder.]

David: Safe!

Han: You're it!

David: I'm safe.

Han: You're not safe. The climbing rock is safe.

David: The climbing rock *used* to be safe. Now it's the tree.

Han: That's against the rules! You can't change safe.

David: Where in the rules does it say you can't change safe?

Han: It's not fair.

David: Life's not fair.

[Han starts to walk away, sulking.]

David: Oh, come on. [letting go of the ladder] There, look. I'm not safe anymore.

Han: I don't want to play.

David: [climbing the ladder] OK, suit yourself… Betcha I can climb higher than you.

Han: Betcha can't.

David: Have you ever gone this high?

Han: Yes.

David: When?

Han: One time.

David: Yeah, right.

[Pause.]

Han: Davie, what are you going to be when you grow up?

David: Me? I'm not going to grow up.

Han: Everybody grows up. So what do you want to be?

David: I'm going to be… a king. That way I can make all the rules and nobody will tell me what to do.

Han: OK, then I'm going to be a king, too.

David: We can't both be king. And anyway, you're a girl.

Han: So?

[Jesse and Samuel enter and stand behind David and Han.]

Jesse: David.

[The characters freeze. The Storyteller speaks to the audience.]

Storyteller/Han: David and Han's father, Jesse. Jesse had an unspoken understanding with his children.

Jesse: Hannah, this is what I expect of you: You will be a good girl. You will be pleasant and polite to strangers. I expect you take care of your brothers. I expect you will cook and keep house. Every once in a while, you will behave emotionally and irrationally. Eventually, you will be married and have children. And although I love you as only a father could, I expect that you won't add up to very much. These are my expectations of you, Hannah, but I'll never tell you that.

Han: Why not?

Jesse: I don't have to… And as for you, David. I expect you to be a boy. I expect you to get into trouble often, to be rebellious, and willful, and cocky. But, at some point, I expect you to understand and accept your responsibilities as a man. I expect you to work hard to make something of yourself. I expect you to be responsible and mature. I expect you to do what's expected of you and to eventually become exactly the same as me, in the way I became the same as my father and he became the same as his father before him.

David: But I want to be a king.

Jesse: You can't be king. We have a king – Saul. Anyway, princes become kings, not shepherds.

David: What do shepherds become?

Jesse: Sheep-owners.

David: Oh.

Storyteller/Han: [to audience] Jesse had a stranger with him.

[Jesse and Samuel approach David.]

Jesse: David, this is the prophet Samuel. He has come all the way from his colony at Ramah, apparently to see you. Do you have any idea why the most powerful holy man in the country should want to see you?

David: No, sir, I don't.

Jesse: [politely] Samuel, not meaning to pry, but perhaps you could…

[Samuel silences Jesse with a look. He stares intently at David. Samuel looks up and over his shoulder, as if checking something, then back at David.]

Samuel: Kneel.

David: Why?

Jesse: Don't talk back, David.

Samuel: Because I have to pour this oil on your head and I don't like lifting my arms any higher than I have to.

[David kneels. Samuel anoints.]

Samuel: What's your name?

David: David?

Samuel: Darren?

David: David.

Samuel: David, you are now the Lord's anointed… Get used to it. Let's go.

[Samuel leaves with David in tow, David looking quite perplexed.]

Storyteller/Han: So, just like that, David left his family and went away with the prophet Samuel.

[Music bridge. Jesse exits. Han moves off to the side, from which she can narrate. Samuel and David are walking. Samuel is grumbling to himself.]

Samuel: [griping] I'm too old for this kind of walking. A man of my age should not be trekking across the whole goddamn country. A little stroll around the property, that's fine. A bit of a hike down the road and into town, I can live with that. But this, this is too much. Do you hear me? Too much!

David: Sir?

Samuel: Who? What? Oh, you. What do you want?

David: I was just wondering… where we're going?

Samuel: [bitter cynicism] That, my son, is on a need-to-know basis. *Everything* is on a need-to-know basis. So there's no point in asking where you're going. No point in asking why. No point in asking what will happen when you get there. No point in asking whether maybe this whole thing might be considered treason and therefore punishable by death, and isn't there somebody else who can do this job instead of sending an old man who has already done more than his fair share of dangerous and stupid things just because God wakes him up in the middle of the night and tells him to do it!

David: I can wait until we get there.

[Samuel is speaking less to David and more to God, whom he locates generally upwards.]

Samuel: Damn right you can wait. And then when the word comes, you're expected to just pack up and go. Just like that. No "Let me just finish this chapter." No "What was that name again?" Just up and out in the middle of the night.

[Samuel "hears" something and then responds.]

Samuel: I know that. You think I don't know that? I'm just saying, does it always have to be the middle of the night? Why not mid-morning, enough time to pack a lunch and check a map? And why not someplace close by, instead of this cross-country adventure?

David: There's a valley up ahead. Is that where we're going?

Samuel: And another thing, you better be sure about *this* one, because I'm not doing this again. I can't handle the… That's not what I'm saying! If you would let me finish my sentence… What? What did you say…? No, I didn't hear it… No, it's because you mumble. You do!

David: Samuel?

Samuel: You slur your words and… My hearing is as good as it's always been, I'll have you know.

David: Samuel.

Samuel: [noticing David] What?

David: A valley.

Samuel: Yes, that's the one. Stay close.

Storyteller: The Valley of Elah. A battlefield.

[Battle music. Saul and the Israelite soldiers enter. Goliath and the Philistine soldiers enter.]

Storyteller: On one side is Saul, king of Israel. On the other side, Goliath, the Philistine shock trooper, a giant at nine-and-a-half feet. And on both sides of the valley are soldiers – normal men with wives and children and parents and friends, who, for various reasons and non-reasons, are preparing themselves to kill or be killed, and all the time wishing to be back home and safe. Meanwhile, Saul is considering his situation carefully, calmly, weighing all his options.

Saul: We're dead. That's it; we're dead. We might as well slit our wrists and lie on the ground and die. Go ahead, take it. It's all yours. I've done everything I'm supposed to do, and it hasn't worked, so just go ahead and take it… What am I doing?! I'm the king. The men look to me for courage. I've got to project strength, confidence, assurance. If I'm scared, they're scared, and then we'll lose for sure… Not that we really stand a chance in hell, because they've got a ten-foot-tall *giant*!

[Goliath makes an announcement.]

Goliath: Slaves of Saul! I'd rather not have to kill you all. Tell your king to send me his best. If he has someone who can kill me, let him come and fight me man-to-man. Otherwise, give yourselves up now and avoid the excess bloodshed.

[Pause. Saul looks at his army. They are all looking at the ground, whistling, shuffling their feet, trying to avoid eye contact. David and Samuel enter.]

David: I'll do it.

Saul: Go away, son. I'm very busy losing a war.

David: I'm serious.

Saul: I don't know who you are, son, but you're too young, you're too small, you're not properly trained, and the man is nine-and-a-half feet tall.

David: I've killed wolves. And bears! Bears can get big.

Saul: Bears don't carry weapons. Now, try to stay out of the way.

Samuel: Let him try, Saul.

Saul: [bitterly] Samuel. What are you doing here?

Samuel: I'm here with the boy.

Saul: You want me to send a boy to do one-on-one battle with a giant. You can't be serious.

Samuel: [to God] Am I serious?… [to Saul] Apparently, I am.

Saul: In case you haven't noticed, sending children to their death isn't great for boosting morale.

Samuel: It's still the popularity contest for you, isn't it.

Saul: Don't tell me how to run a war. I know how to run a war. I'm not some beginner, learning strategy from a textbook. I've fought, I've killed, I know what works. And sending little boys to fight giants doesn't work. It's just not done!

David: You mean because it's never been done.

Saul: Exactly.

David: Does that mean you shouldn't try it now?

Saul: Yes!

Samuel: You have no one who can defeat the shock trooper.

Saul: The rules say that young boys cannot beat giants.

Samuel: Saul, you're outnumbered and outclassed. If you play by the rules you will lose, and you know it.

Saul: I'll send in my best fighter. Jonathan. My son Jonathan is the best we have. I'll send him in, and with any luck... [realizing] Oh God, I can't send my son! Help me put my armor on. I'm going myself.

    [Saul puts on armor.]

Samuel: Don't be stupid.

Saul: I'm not stupid! I'm a good fighter, aren't I? Haven't I won my share of battles?

Samuel: Yes.

Saul: So I could win. I could actually stand a chance of beating him. Right? Come on, you're the prophet. Tell me if I can beat their giant or not.

Samuel: Does it take a prophet to see that he's ten feet tall, and you're not?

Saul: What are you saying?

Samuel: I'm saying he'll walk on your face.

    [Pause. Saul looks at David doubtfully.]

Saul: I can't see this working.

Samuel: You will be surprised.

Saul: [giving in] Help me get this boy into armor.

    [Samuel and Saul start loading David with armor.]

Saul: This isn't the way you fight a war, you know. You don't send a boy against a giant. It's against all the rules of war, and it doesn't make any sense.

Storyteller: Meanwhile, Goliath patiently waited for an opponent.

Goliath: [to audience] I'm not violent by nature. My name is Goliath. I was born in a small village. My parents were weavers, fairly short people both of them, so when by the age of eight I was standing six-foot-five, everyone knew I was a bit of a freak. My mother wove lovely patterned rugs and as a child I always wanted to help. But of course my hands were too large and clumsy. Children wouldn't play with me. Adults showed me more fear than love... I never had any great desire to be a fighter, but when you're as tall as I am, you soon realize that the only things you're good for are killing people and reaching things from high shelves. So I became the most feared shock trooper of the Philistine army. Killing is what's expected of me. I'm nine-and-a-half feet tall, what else can I do?

Storyteller: David was finally outfitted with the appropriate armor and weapons.

Saul: How does that feel?

[David is completely covered with heavy armor, piled high.]

David: [muffled] I can't move.

Saul: You're probably not used to it. Try taking a step.

[David takes two clattery steps and then collapses.]

Saul: This doesn't inspire confidence.

David: Get me out of here.

[Samuel and Saul extract him from the pile of armor.]

Saul: I told you this wouldn't work.

David: Look, why don't I do it without armor?

[Saul gives David a blank look.]

David: When I'm in my father's field, protecting the sheep, I don't wear armor and a sword. I use a leather sling and some stones.

Saul: Battles aren't fought with slings and stones.

David: Exactly! But look at Goliath. Not only is he a giant, he's an experienced fighter. He knows how to defend against swords and spears and armor. And no matter how good I could be, he'd be better. All the rules are on his side, and if I play by his rules, I'll lose for sure. But what if I change the rules. He's *expecting* a trained opponent, all loaded up with this stuff. But does he know how to deal with a kid, traveling light, who's a super shot with the sling?

Saul: No! That's it. I'm putting my foot down. It's bad enough that we're sending a boy to do a man's work, but to send him unarmed and unprepared. It's insane.

David: When the rules are against you, change the rules. Go for the unexpected. Try the thing that's never been tried before.

Saul: And if it doesn't work?

David: If you don't risk, you don't win.

Samuel: Here are five stones, David. God will be with you.

Saul: Excuse me, I haven't approved this yet.

Samuel: Off you go.

Saul: [sarcastic] Am I still king? Has there been a coup I haven't been told about?

Samuel: We'll talk about that later.

Storyteller: The battlefield falls silent as David and Goliath face each other.

Goliath: [gently] Hello.

David: Hello.

Goliath: Are you ready to fight?

David: Yes.

Goliath: I don't think you're properly outfitted for this.

David: I have everything I'll need.

Goliath: You're a brave young man. No one would think less of you if you backed out now.

David: I'm not afraid.

Goliath: You understand that this is to the death?

David: I do.

Goliath: And you know what that means?

David: As much as anyone can.

Goliath: And you're sure you still want to do this?

David: I'm sure.

Goliath: I'm sorry to hear that… Well, our friends are expecting some blood. Shall we get started?

> [David pulls out his sling and spins it. The sound of a whirring sling, the whistle of rock through air, a smack, a crunch.]

All: [gasp]

Goliath: [quietly] Ah, now that's a nice pattern.

> [Goliath falls and is caught by the Philistines.]

All: [cheer]

> [Israelites, Philistines, and Samuel exit.]

Saul: You're lucky, son. But you're also talented. I like lucky, talented people. Can you play a musical instrument?

David: I play harp.

Saul: You're just the kind of person I need. I want you to come with me and live at the royal court.

[Saul hands David a guitar.]

Storyteller: And that's the story of how David went from shepherd to hero.

[David plays guitar, as the playing area is set up for Part 2.]

SCENE 2: THE REBEL

[Music]

Storyteller: David is now a young man with a place at the royal court as King Saul's harp-player. Everyone at the palace likes David. Especially Saul's son, Jonathan.

[David and Jonathan enter.]

David: Is your father always like that?

Jonathan: Like what?

David: You know, the mood swings. One minute he's your best friend and everything's happy, and the next minute he's sure the world is out to get him.

Jonathan: That's just how he is. It's no big deal. He just worries about things too much.

David: I was just wondering if he's upset about…us.

Jonathan: He's probably just nervous about how it looks. He has this thing about what people think.

David: What do people think?

[Jonathan shrugs.]

David: Does your father tell you what to do?

Jonathan: No.

David: Never? He never makes you follow rules?

Jonathan: Wouldn't matter, I do pretty much what I want anyway. And so far it's worked out fine.

David: So, if he thought this was wrong, he wouldn't necessarily tell you.

[Pause.]

Jonathan: Do you think it's wrong?

David: No.

Jonathan: Well then...

David: It's just that...

Jonathan: Look. I love you. Do you love me?

David: Yes.

Jonathan: There we go then. What are we going to do?

David: I'm just wondering if it's right.

Jonathan: I haven't seen it written anywhere that it's not.

David: I have.

Jonathan: You can't legislate love, David. Maybe that's why it scares people so much. If you can control love you can control anything. I'm not going to change how I feel just because someone says I should.

David: Even your father?

Jonathan: My father worries about doing the right thing. Always, "What am I supposed to do?" Never, "What do I *want* to do?" It's like he's trying to win some sort of prize for following the rules.

David: So, should I be worried about your father?

Jonathan: No, of course not. He likes you. He really does. I don't even think he really knows that we're...

[Saul interrupts the story. Jonathan and David freeze. Saul speaks to the Storyteller. David and Jonathan exit.]

Saul: OK, stop it!

Storyteller: What's the matter?

Saul: I don't like this. I don't like what you're doing to this story. You're making us all look bad.

Storyteller: Me? How am I doing that?

Saul: Don't play dumb with me, missy. You know full well what you're doing. And it's sick.

Storyteller: I still don't know what you're talking about.

Saul: You are taking the story and introducing…things that don't belong.

Storyteller: Are you talking about David and Jonathan?

Saul: There *is* no David and Jonathan! There's a David, and there's a Jonathan, but there's no DavidandJonathan.

Storyteller: We're just telling a story.

Saul: You're twisting the story. Now, the stories you tell in the privacy of your own home are not my concern. But when you come out in public and, for whatever reasons – sensationalism or slander – start making these kind of implications, then I have to step in and take action.

Storyteller: Why does this bother you so much?

Saul: It doesn't bother me.

Storyteller: It certainly seems to bother you.

Saul: I just don't like the suggestion that things like *that* go on in my palace.

Storyteller: Why do you care?

Saul: Because it reflects on me. Because the whole country is watching me. God is watching me. And if it looks like I'm not doing the correct things, I will lose my throne and everything I've spent my whole life working for.

Storyteller: You don't really believe that, do you?

Saul: It wouldn't surprise me if he's doing it on purpose. Just to make me look bad.

Storyteller: Who?

Saul: David. He wants what I've got. He wants to take everything away from me.

Storyteller: I think you're a bit paranoid.

Saul: Just move on to another part of the story!

Storyteller: Will the scene in the throne room do?

Saul: That will do fine.

Storyteller: [to audience] That night David went to play the harp for Saul.

[David enters. David is playing guitar.]

Saul: David.

David: Sir?

Saul: What do you think a king is, David?

David: A king is someone who rules the country, and makes laws, and commands armies, and...

Saul: Do you think I'm a good king?

David: You've been very good to me.

Saul: But in general, do you think I'm a good king?

David: I suppose.

Saul: Do you think you could do better?

David: I haven't really thought about it.

Saul: Oh come on. You must have at least *thought* about it.

David: Not really.

Saul: [under his breath] Liar.

David: Sorry, sir?

Saul: You're so young and charming, David. Everybody likes you... But I hear what you say about me behind my back.

David: I don't.

Saul: I may not always be right, but I'm the king. Do you hear me? *I'm* the king!

David: I think you need some rest, sir.

Saul: [more calmly] You're right. Help me up.

[David goes to help Saul up, but Saul throws him to the ground and tries to drive a spear into him. David rolls out of the way in time.]

Saul: Traitor!

[David runs out.]

Saul: Wait! David, I'm sorry. Come back. Come back!

Storyteller: David ran to Jonathan and told him that his father had tried to kill him. Jonathan found it hard to believe, but went to check it out.

[Jonathan casually walks up to Saul. Saul is also playing it cool.]

Jonathan: Father.

Saul: Jonathan.

Jonathan: Lovely evening.

Saul: Yes, very nice.

[Pause.]

Saul: So, where is your little friend this evening?

Jonathan: Who?

Saul: You know, the fellow with the harp.

Jonathan: David?

Saul: Yes, David, that's it. Where's he at tonight?

Jonathan: Oh. Well, he had to go back home for a couple of weeks. Some sort of sudden family thing.

Saul: Nothing serious, I hope.

Jonathan: Oh, no, I don't think so.

Saul: Where is home again for him?

Jonathan: He told me, you know, but I don't remember. Why?

Saul: No reason. I just love the way he plays the harp. Any chance you could talk him into coming back early?

Jonathan: I don't think so.

Saul: You're sure.

Jonathan: Yeah, I'm sure.

[Pause. Jonathan and Saul look at each other. They both know what's going on. Jonathan turns to leave.]

Saul: Where are you going?

Jonathan: Out.

Saul: Oh, why don't you stay. We haven't talked in so long.

[Jonathan doesn't respond.]

Saul: You're just like your mother, you know that! Rebellious and perverse and not thinking about the future!

Jonathan: What does the future have to do with it?

Saul: It's your future I'm thinking about. Don't you want to become king some day?

Jonathan: You know that I've never cared about that.

Saul: I only want what's best for you.

Jonathan: Oh stop it.

Saul: Jonathan, I'm your father, and I'm giving you a direct order. Don't go out there, to that traitor… Stay here with me. Everything you need is right here.

Jonathan: I'll be back later.

[Jonathan moves away from Saul. Saul watches him leave.]

Storyteller: Jonathan went out to the south field where David was hiding behind a pile of stones. David and Jonathan had arranged a signal. If David had misinterpreted the situation and everything was safe, Jonathan would shoot short of the stones. But if it was not safe, Jonathan would shoot over David's head.

Saul: Jonathan! [softly] I'm your father.

[Jonathan places an "arrow" in his bow, pulls back, and releases. David watches the "arrow" go over his head. David and Jonathan look at each other and exit in opposite directions.]

Storyteller: So David fled to Ramah, the home of Samuel and his band of prophets.

[The cast becomes a band of prophets, singing and spinning dervish-like. David enters.]

David: I need Samuel's help!

Prophet: Samuel is dead. We're mourning and celebrating his passing.

David: King Saul is chasing me. He thinks I'm a threat.

[The prophets stop and focus on David.]

Prophet: You're in serious trouble, David. This isn't a wolf that's chasing you, or even a giant. This is a king, and kings have armies, and weapons, and spies. Kings have power, and a tendency to get what they want.

David: What can I do? He's coming after me.

Prophet: You'll have to go through "the well" into exile.

David: Through the well?

Prophet: Saul won't want to follow you that way. First of all, start turning around.

David: Why?

Prophet: Just do it.

      [David starts to spin.]

Prophet: Keep going.

      [David starts to spin. The prophets chant quietly.]

Prophet: Now listen to my voice. Can you hear me?

David: Yes.

Prophet: The world is falling away from under your feet. Everything you knew is dropping away. Let it go.

David: Why?

Prophet: Because you can't take it with you into exile. It will slow you down. Let go of the laws you lived by. Let go of your hopes for power and success. Let go of your need for security and comfort. You're no longer a hero of the royal court, you're an outlaw. The only way to escape is if you're willing to let go of everything you had and hoped to have. Can you feel it falling away?

David: Yes, I can!

Prophet: Good. Now look at your feet. Can you see a well?

David: Yes, I see it! It's very dark.

Prophet: And very deep, and nothing goes through it unchanged. Your escape is through that well, and exile on the other side. Are you ready?

David: Yes.

Prophet: Then jump.

      [David closes his eyes and jumps. All freeze. The scene becomes a camp, and the prophets change into exiles.]

Storyteller: From Ramah, David fled south and went into hiding. As rumors of David's exile spread, people came from all over the country to join him. There soon gathered around David a whole army of outlaws, all of them exiles in their own right. Some were people too poor to pay their debts. Some were people shunned by their villages. Some were simply people who had said the wrong thing to the wrong person. And although, to normal society, they were all malcontents and misfits, in the exile they were a community.

[One of the exiles lets out a loud belch.]

Exile 1: I still say it's wrong.

Exile 2: It's not wrong.

Exile 1: It's wrong to steal.

Exile 2: We're outlaws. We need to eat. How are we going to get food if we don't steal it?

Exile 1: We seek donations. We trade services.

Exile 2: We tried that. We asked him to give us his goats and we would pay him when we got some money.

Exile 3: As soon as some very rich person joins us in exile…

Exile 2: And he said no, so now we have to steal them.

Exile 1: It's his right to say no. They're *his* goats.

Exile 2: But why are they his goats? Why his and not mine or yours? What has he done to deserve to have goats, while we're hungry?

Exile 1: David, what do you say?

David: I say, goat sounds good to me.

Exile 2: Exactly. Why is stealing wrong? Because the people who own things that could get stolen make the rules. The law says it's wrong for someone to try to kill the king, but it's perfectly all right for the king to try to kill David. That's because the king makes the rules. The law always benefits the rich and the powerful, and that's why people like us end up in exile.

Exile 1: So, David, you're saying it's all right to steal?

David: I'm saying it's getting close to supper time, and I'm hungry.

Exile 2: And that's another thing. Why do we eat at roughly the same times every day? Who decided that? Shouldn't we just eat whenever we feel like it? Who benefits from making us structure our lives around regular meals?

Exile 4: OK, here's a question: Imagine that we're hiding out in a cave. All right? And King Saul is out hunting for us.

Exile 3: Can I play Saul?

Exile 4: And say, just say, that Saul happens to walk into this cave without seeing us.

Exile 3: [as Saul] Oh boy, am I stuffed! I sure didn't need that second side of beef, but, oh, the white wine and mushroom sauce…

[Exile 3 ("Saul") squats down and hikes up his robe.]

Exile 1: [disgusted] Oh please.

Exile 4: All right, all right. So this is the situation. Here's Saul, totally vulnerable. What do you do?

[Pause.]

Exile 1: All right, here's what I'd do. [to "Saul"] Your highness. I'm sorry to…interrupt you, but I need to tell you that your persecution of us is unwarranted. We are all good and faithful citizens who want nothing more than…

"Saul": Yes, I see your point. Now see mine.

Exile 1: [being stabbed] Hyahgk!

["Saul" stabs Exile 1. Exile 1 moves off to the side.]

Exile 3: Next!

Exile 5: OK, how about this.

Exile 5: [putting a knife to "Saul's" throat] All right, Saul. One false move and you're dead. Your rules are unfair, and I don't like you oppressing me and my friends. Now you either call off your dogs, or I'll ventilate your throat.

"Saul": I don't deal with terrorists.

Exile 5: Well, you better start trying, or we'll roll you out of this cave in two pieces.

"Saul": OK, OK! Just tell me what you want.

Exile 5: [taking the knife away] Well, first of all – Hyahgk!

["Saul" runs Exile 5 through. Exile 5 moves off to the side.]

Exile 2: All right, back off. This is how you do it… King Saul?

"Saul": Yes… Hyahgk!

[Exile 2 stabs "Saul." He dies.]

Exile 2: Right?

Exile 4: David, what would you do?

David: Me…? I would sneak up behind him, very quietly, and without his knowing it, I would cut off the back of his robe. And then sometime later, I would show it to him.

Exile 2: Why would you do that? That's stupid!

David: I don't know, it's just what I'd do. Just to let him know that I'm still around.

Exile 2: But that would just make him madder and more determined to kill you.

[David shrugs.]

David: You might be right.

Exile 2: I worry about you.

[David and exiles exit. Saul enters.]

Storyteller: So for months Saul hunted David and David always stayed one step ahead of him. Saul knew that if David didn't have a reason to want the throne before, he did now. And what's more, he had a good chance at succeeding.

[David enters and hands Saul a scrap of cloth, smiles, and leaves. Saul spins around to find a hole cut in the back of his clothes. Meanwhile, the Storyteller puts on a shawl or cloak, becoming a witch of Endor.]

Storyteller: So Saul, desperately trying to understand why everything was falling away from him, put on a disguise and went to Endor to consult a witch.

[Saul puts on a cloak to disguise himself. Eerie music.]

Witch: Enter stranger. Do I know you?

Saul: No. No, I'm just a…hunter.

Witch: [slyly] A hunter, but not a catcher, I'm thinking.

Saul: Can you summon a spirit from the dead?

Witch: "Can" is one thing. "Should" is another. You know that summoning the dead is illegal.

Saul: I know.

Witch: There are laws. Rules and regulations. That kind of witchcraft is not to be done.

Saul: I know. Do it anyway.

Witch: I could be killed.

Saul: I'll take responsibility. Just do it.

Witch: [incanting] Give me a space, an empty space, and a long path from Sheol. And loan me a dead man's voice, for only a moment. Send him down that path and let him speak to us.

    [The spirit of Samuel enters.]

Saul: Samuel!

Samuel: [irritated] What? What do you want?

Saul: Can I talk to him?

    [The witch nods.]

Saul: Samuel, it's Saul. What did I do wrong? Why is David evading me?

Samuel: This is what you called me for?

Saul: You anointed me king. I was God's chosen one. And I've worked hard to live up to that. So why isn't it working? Why is David succeeding?

Samuel: Because David is the Lord's anointed. Not you. I anointed him before you even met him. You may have the wealth, and the soldiers, and the crown, but you haven't been king for years. Give it up.

Saul: You anointed another man king while I was wearing the crown? How could you do that?

Samuel: What are you going to do, kill me? I'm dead!

Saul: But what am I supposed to do? I want to be king.

Samuel: It's over, Saul. Go home… And don't call me anymore. I'm retired.

Saul: But this isn't fair.

Samuel: Saul, just so you know… God plays favorites.

    [The spirit of Samuel exits. Saul crumbles to the ground. The witch offers him a bowl of soup.]

Witch: Here. You should eat something.

Saul: [in despair] No, no.

Witch: Yes. Eat… You're disappointed.

[She helps him up. He sips from the bowl.]

Saul: My father told me, "Saul, be good. Do what you're told. Follow the rules and you will be rewarded. Play the game well and you will be a winner. You can be rich, you can be powerful… You can be happy, just do the right things. But if you break the rules, you'll be punished. Nobody wants to be punished, so play by the rules." He told me that. But I'm not happy… He should have told me that God plays favorites.

Witch: So what are you going to do?

[Saul shrugs.]

Saul: I'm going to hunt down David and I'm going to kill him.

Witch: Do you think that will work?

[Saul looks at the witch sadly. He exits. The Storyteller takes off the cloak.]

Storyteller: The next day Saul went into battle against the Philistines.

[Battle music. The sounds of swords clashing. Saul enters fighting.]

Storyteller: Saul fought like a madman. He never stopped fighting, because if he stopped he would have time to think about his failure, about how, despite his hard work, his struggle to keep in control, and his faithful following of the rules, he had lost it all. And he couldn't face that, so he kept on fighting. It was only a matter of time before he was mortally wounded.

Saul: Aagh!

Soldier: My lord, you're wounded. Let me carry you out of here so you can be treated.

Saul: No! I'm OK. I can still fight.

Soldier: Sir, for your own good…

Saul: Leave me alone!

[A messenger enters.]

Messenger: [panting] Sir, I have a message for you. Your son, Jonathan, has been… He's dead. On the south side of Gilboa. His group fought bravely, but they were outnumbered.

Saul: So. That's it then.

[He waves the messenger off. The messenger exits.]

Saul: Soldier.

Soldier: Sir?

Saul: Kill me.

Soldier: What?

Saul: I don't want them to take my life.

Soldier: I won't kill you, sir.

Saul: I'm your king and that's an order. Kill me.

Soldier: My job is to *protect* the king.

Saul: [pathetically] Please.

Soldier: [disgusted] Do it yourself.

[The soldier drops his spear at Saul's feet and exits.]

Storyteller: So he did.

[Saul props himself on the spear and falls. The sounds of battle stop. Pause.]

Storyteller: David mourned for Jonathan. And strangely enough, he mourned for Saul as well. He wept for them. He cried; he sang. He tried to make up metaphors for them. They were like eagles and like lions, like swords and like arrows, but nothing seemed to fit. The best that David could say was this:

David: The mighty have fallen.

[David picks up the crown.]

Storyteller: And that's the story of how David went from outlaw to king.

[David puts the crown on his head. Music.]

[INTERMISSION]

SCENE 3: THE RULE-MAKER

[Intro music. The cast enters.]

Storyteller: David is now an adult, and a king.

All: [cheer] David! David! David!

[Enter David, followed by Joab. David climbs the ladder and waves graciously at his adoring public.]

Storyteller: He has brought together the warring factions within the country, made a unified Israel with Jerusalem as its center, and with the help of Joab, his general, has expanded Israel's territory.

David: Joab, who have we beaten so far?

Joab: [checking a list] The Philistines, the Moabites, the Edomites, and the Syrians.

David: Who does that leave?

Joab: [checking] The Ammonites?

David: Let's go.

Joab: Yes, sir.

[The cast marches off. David starts to march off with them. Joab stops him.]

Joab: Where do you think you're going…sir?

David: West, Joab, west. We'll show those Ammonites who's who.

Joab: "We" is not the proper pronoun, sir.

David: I'm the king, Joab. I have to go.

Joab: No, sir. You're the king; you have to stay. If anything were to happen to you…

David: Nothing's going to happen to me.

Joab: *If* something were to happen to you, it would have a negative effect on the whole country.

David: But if I don't go and fight, everyone will think I'm a coward.

Joab: No, they will think you're a king, who is responsible and acts in the best interests of his country.

David: But I'm a good fighter. I always win.

Joab: We have other good fighters, who are more expendable than you… I'm your general, David. It is my job to do what needs to be done to keep you in power, to win your wars, and to protect your person. This is my area of expertise; I make the rules here. Is that understood…sir?

David: I had more fun when I was in exile.

Joab: I'm sure you did.

[Joab exits. Pause. David climbs the ladder. Pause.]

David: [to himself] Fine. I'll just stay here, and *be responsible*… But doesn't it make sense, though, that a king should be able to do whatever he wants? I mean, what's the point in being king if you still have to go by somebody else's rules? I mean… Right, OK, never mind… I'll just sit here looking out over the city. Who knows, maybe something exciting will happen. Maybe… Whoa.

[Bathsheba appears, drying herself off with a towel.]

Storyteller: The woman in the bathtub was Bathsheba and, by the standards of the time, she was *very* beautiful. Now, there are some laws that are more…biological than ethical, and…and David found himself gripped by just such a law. He sent someone to get the woman and bring her up to the palace.

David: [to audience] It may not be right, but hey, I'm the king. And anyway, *everybody* does it.

[Bathsheba wraps herself in the towel.]

Storyteller: Now Bathsheba's husband was a man named Uriah. He was a Hittite, which means he was considered a foreigner in Israel, an immigrant and an outsider. I don't know if that's important to the story. What is important is that Uriah was a soldier in David's army, fighting for him in the land of Ammon.

[Uriah enters.]

Uriah: [to audience] Sometimes my homeland I miss, but this I tell you – I love Israel. Proud am I to live here and to be soldier of King David. Lucky and blessed I think myself, to have an adopted home I am proud of, a wonderful job, and a beautiful wife. A better life I cannot imagine.

Joab: Soldier!

Uriah: Uriah, sir. Uriah the Hittite.

Joab: Uriah, we need men on the east flank.

Uriah: [eagerly] Yes sir!

[Uriah and Joab exit. Bathsheba approaches David's ladder.]

Storyteller: Meanwhile, back at the palace, Bathsheba had arrived.

David: [charmingly] Hello.

> [Bathsheba nods. Music. A bedsheet is draped over the ladder. David leads Bathsheba behind this screen. Pause. From behind, the towel is draped over the top of the ladder. With David and Bathsheba out of sight, the Storyteller is left alone on the stage.]

Storyteller: [uncomfortably] Well… Here we are.

> [An occasional giggle might be heard from behind the ladder/screen. The Storyteller looks around for something distracting to do or talk about. She points at something vague.]

Storyteller: Oh, that's a, that's an…interesting…thing.

> [The Storyteller tries to whistle a bit, then stops.]

Storyteller: [killing time] Well, while we're waiting for this story to get going again, why don't I just summarize what's already happened, in case you missed the first parts. It all started off with David and his little sister in their father's sheep field. And then Samuel came along and…with the oil, and "What was that all about?" And then Goliath, and the stone, and falling, and he wanted to be a weaver but his hands were too big. And then Saul liked David, and Jonathan liked David, and David liked Jonathan, but then Saul didn't like David. And the spear, and yikes! And running and hiding. And then calling the spirit of Samuel up from the dead, and "Leave me alone. David's going to be king." And then Saul got killed, and David became king. And he was a very successful king, but he had to stay home when the army went off to war, and… Oh. I guess you know that part… So… Most people don't know this, but Middle Eastern architecture in this period had houses built around a central courtyard, which was left open to the sky. Which is why David was able to look down from the roof of his palace, which would have been much higher, and see Bathsheba having a bath in her courtyard. You see, it's not like she was having a bath in the streets or anything. Um, another thing you might not know is that bathing…

> [The towel is pulled back behind the ladder. David and Bathsheba come out from behind the screen. Bathsheba exits. The Storyteller heaves a relieved sigh.]

Storyteller: Thank God… Bathsheba returned to her home and David returned to the affairs of state.

> [The Storyteller slips into a cloak and becomes the prophet, Nathan.]

David: Ah, what to do now? Maybe I should build a temple. A place where everybody could come and worship God. A really impressive stone thing…

Storyteller/Nathan: Which is when the prophet Nathan arrived at the royal court… [as Nathan] What does God need with a temple, David?

David: Don't you think God would want a temple? We could do up a good one. We've got the resources.

Nathan: God will not be held. Not by stone walls and curtains. Not by images and symbols. Not by books and words.

David: It was just an idea. Who are you, again?

Nathan: I call myself Nathan. I'm a prophet.

David: Nathan. Do I know you?

Nathan: I don't know. Do you?

David: I guess not. But I like you. Stay as long as you like. You're welcome to…

[Bathsheba enters and clears her throat.]

David: [to Nathan] Excuse me. [to Bathsheba] Yes?

Bathsheba: I'm pregnant.

[Slight pause. Bathsheba exits.]

David: She didn't have very many lines, did she.

Storyteller/Nathan: But she made the ones she had count.

[The Storyteller takes the cloak off and steps off to the side.]

David: [beginning to panic] Oh boy. Oh boy-oh-boy. Pregnant. What am I going to do? This is a scandal, this is; this is not good. This is not… OK. OK, I can handle this. Just stop and think it through. I mean, I'm David, right? I always win. Why is that? Because I'm clever. I play by my own rules. Just like with Goliath. This is just another puzzle. All I need to do is find the creative solution, and… There we go! Easy as that. [calling] Joab.

[Joab enters.]

Joab: Sir.

David: Joab, how's the war going?

Joab: Well enough.

David: Good. Um, Uriah the Hittite…

Joab: Yes, sir?

David: Could you send him home for a couple of days.

Joab: Any reason?

David: Let's just say I need to see him.

Joab: Whatever you say, sir. [Joab exits.]

Storyteller: So Uriah, the husband of Bathsheba, left the battlefield and went to the royal palace.

[Uriah enters.]

David: Uriah!

Uriah: Uriah the Hittite, reporting as ordered, sir!

David: Great… At ease. So, Uriah, how's my old friend Joab doing? Keeping you boys in line?

Uriah: Joab is a wonderful general, sir. To serve under him is my honor.

David: I'm glad to hear that. So the war's going well?

Uriah: Excellent progress we are making, sir. The city of Rabbah we will have captured by the end of the week.

David: Wonderful. And the soldiers are in good spirits?

Uriah: Very good spirits, sir.

David: Good. That's really all I wanted to know.

Uriah: Very good, sir.

David: Thanks for your time, Uriah. I guess you've got the evening off now, don't you.

Uriah: Sir?

David: I hear you have a wife.

Uriah: Bathsheba, sir.

David: You probably haven't seen her for a couple of months, have you.

Uriah: No, sir.

David: That must be hard, spending so much time away from your wife. I guess you'd have a lot of catching up to do.

Uriah: Sir.

David: Well, then, on your way, soldier.

Uriah: Thank you, sir.

Storyteller: So Uriah the Hittite left King David. But he didn't go to his home and he didn't go to his wife. He slept by the door to the king's palace.

>   [Uriah lies in front of the ladder and sleeps. He snores. David nudges him with his foot.]

David: Uriah.

Uriah: [waking at attention] Sir!

David: What are you doing here? You have a house. You have a *wife*.

Uriah: I thought I should sleep here, sir, to protect you in case of attack, sir.

David: That's good of you, Uriah, but I have guards. And you have a wife you probably want to get reacquainted with. Right? So off you go.

>   [Uriah doesn't exit.]

David: Uriah!

Uriah: Sir!

David: You're not going home.

Uriah: Sir?

David: Don't you like your wife?

Uriah: Very much, sir.

>   [Pause. David grabs two bowls.]

David: Are you a drinking man, Uriah?

Uriah: Not while I'm on duty, sir.

David: You're not on duty, Uriah. And it's against policy to refuse a drink when your king is offering.

Uriah: Very well, sir.

>   [They drink.]

David: Very good. Again.

>   [They drink again.]

Storyteller: Many hours and many drinks later...

David: [slightly drunk] How are you feeling, Uriah?

Uriah: [very drunk] Very well, sir!

David: How about that wife of yours?

Uriah: How about her, sir!

David: Don't you think maybe you should go home and…you know. There's duty and then there's *duty*, soldier.

Uriah: It's just that…

David: [slightly frantic] What? What? What could possibly be wrong with taking an evening to sleep with your own wife? What?

Uriah: Well…forgive, sir, but it does not seem right. My general and all of our soldiers are sleeping in an open field. They are cold and maybe tomorrow they get killed. And, well, it does not seem right that in my own bed I should relax and sleep, and to my wife make love, when all my friends are suffering for the sake of their country…sir.

David: Look, Uriah, don't think about that, OK. Now, I'm giving you an order, as your king. Go home. Sleep with your wife. Take it easy. Understand? That's an order.

Uriah: If you say so, sir.

David: I do say so. Now, let me help you to the door. There you go. Now have a good time. I don't want to see you until morning.

Uriah: Yes sir.

> [The drunken Uriah stumbles forward a couple of steps, then collapses to the ground, unconscious.]

David: Uriah?… Uriah!… [frustrated] All right. On to Plan B.

Storyteller: The next day, David sent Uriah back to the front. He also sent word to Joab, his general.

> [Uriah exits. Joab enters.]

David: Joab, I need a favor.

Joab: What.

David: I want you to send Uriah the Hittite into the hot spot, somewhere where the fighting is really heavy.

Joab: …OK.

David: Then I want you to pull your men back, so Uriah gets boxed in.

[Slight pause.]

Joab: You want me to set it up so Uriah gets killed.

David: Can you do it?

Joab: I can do it, but…

David: What?

Joab: I want it in writing.

[Pause.]

David: You've got it.

Storyteller: So Joab sent Uriah the Hittite into the thick of battle. And Uriah went, because he trusted his general, his country, and his king.

[A battlefield set up like a chessboard. Uriah moves according to Joab's instructions.]

Joab: Uriah to Rabbah six.

Uriah: Yes sir.

[Uriah moves and does battle.]

Joab: Uriah to Rabbah four.

Uriah: Yes sir.

[Uriah moves and does battle.]

Joab: Uriah to Rabbah nine.

Uriah: Yes sir.

[Uriah moves and does battle.]

Joab: [coolly] Uriah to Rabbah one.

[Uriah starts to move, then hesitates.]

Uriah: Sir. Do you not mean Rabbah eight, sir?

Joab: Uriah to Rabbah one.

Uriah: Yes sir.

[Uriah moves and is slaughtered.]

Uriah: [dying] Aaagh!

[Pause. Finally the actors playing Uriah and Joab exit in silence.]

David: Yes! The golden boy wins again! Mister problem-solver! Mister creative solution! Ha, ha, ha. Now, all I need to do is give Bathsheba a short period of mourning, then bring her to the palace and marry her. No scandal. No awkward embarrassment. All because of cleverness and clear thinking.

Storyteller: Then the prophet Nathan returned.

[The Storyteller puts the Nathan cloak back on.]

Nathan: King David.

David: [trying to remember the name] …Nathan! How are you doing?

Nathan: I need your advice.

David: Well, I'm on a roll these days. Shoot.

Nathan: How would you rule in this situation?

[Music. Two sheep owners, a lamb, and a visitor enter.]

Nathan: A rich man and a poor man live in the same town. The rich man has hundreds of sheep, and everything he could possibly need. The poor man only has, or rather had, one little ewe lamb…

Lamb: Baaa…

Nathan: …Which he loved and treated like one of his children. I say "had" because a few days ago a traveler came to visit the rich man.

Visitor: Simon, you old fig-eating jackal, how are you doing?

Rich Man: Eli, you old sand-hating camel, what have you been up to?

Visitor: Oh, this and that.

Rich Man: Good. Come on in and take a load off.

Visitor: Don't mind if I do. Come to think of it, I'm feeling a bit peckish.

Rich Man: Well, let's see what I can scrounge up.

Nathan: The rich man wanted to serve mutton, but rather than slaughter one of his own sheep, he took the poor man's ewe lamb and served it to his visitor.

[The rich man takes the lamb and twists its neck.]

Lamb: [dying] Baagh.

[The sheep owners, lamb, and visitor exit.]

Nathan: So, wise King David, what would you do?

David: That's awful! Did that really happen…? That rich man deserves to die. What an unfeeling bastard! Give me his name. I'll make sure he compensates the other fellow for his sheep. Who is this man?

Nathan: You are that man.

[Pause.]

David: OK, well played. You really sucked me in on that one. Did you know that I have a soft spot for sheep, or was that just a lucky guess…? Let's cut to the chase. What are you telling me?

Nathan: That you have sinned.

David: OK…

Nathan: And that has consequences.

David: No, really.

Nathan: I'm serious.

David: But I'm David. I mean…*I'm David*. I'm the golden boy. I can do no wrong.

Nathan: You believe that, don't you?

David: So, what? God doesn't like me anymore?

Nathan: That's not what I said.

David: You said "consequences." What does that mean? That I'm going to be punished? Because I slept with somebody else's wife? Everybody does that! Is God suddenly deciding to crack down on that sort of thing?

Nathan: Just because you're king doesn't mean you can do whatever you want.

David: Everybody seems to be telling me that these days.

Nathan: And it doesn't mean you're above the law.

David: I make the law. How can I not be above it?

Nathan: God has laws, too.

David: Oh come on. Do you really expect me to believe that God spends all day sitting up on some cloud watching me, and checking this little rule book? And when I do something wrong, zap, here comes a lightning bolt, or a plague…or an annoying prophet with pathetic little sheep stories.

Nathan: God isn't up there keeping score! [tapping his own chest, and then David's] God is in here, and in there, and in between. And God's law is all around us. And the deepest of God's laws is this: Everything is connected.

David: Everything is connected.

Nathan: You forgot that. You acted like your actions wouldn't affect anyone else. You treated people like pawns. This isn't a game. This isn't a challenge to your creativity. You didn't just have a fling. You changed someone's life forever. You ended a life. You made the world worse, not better.

David: And so God is going to punish me.

Nathan: God doesn't have to punish you, David. Everything is connected. Your actions come full circle. Everything has changed, and your house will feel the effect of your sin.

David: I don't need this. I don't care if you are a prophet.

Nathan: I'm just bringing the message, David.

David: All right, I'm guilty. Message received. Now get out of here.

Nathan: You're not guilty, David. You're responsible.

David: Go!

Nathan: Everything is connected, David.

David: Get out, now!

[The Storyteller takes the cloak off.]

Storyteller: So the prophet Nathan left. And in the years that followed, the house of David was never at peace. That's the end of that story.

[Music.]

SCENE 4: THE FATHER

[Music. David sits on top of the ladder.]

Storyteller: David has been king for many years and he is quite comfortable. Over the years, his family has grown quite large. Perhaps a quick roll call would be useful.

[Amnon, Tamar, Absalom, and Solomon enter.]

Amnon: I'm Amnon, the oldest son of David.

Storyteller: David's firstborn and heir to the throne. David has a soft spot for him.

Tamar: My name is Tamar, daughter of David, stepsister to Amnon.

Storyteller: Tamar is a wise girl, and beautiful.

Absalom: Absalom, David's son, Tamar's brother, Amnon's stepbrother.

Storyteller: A good-looking young man. Notice his wonderful head of long flowing hair. He's quite proud of it… In many ways, Absalom is very much like his father.

Solomon: My name is Solomon. My other name is Jedidiah. It means "beloved of God" in Hebrew. I am David's son, and…everybody else's stepbrother.

Storyteller: Solomon's still quite young, but always reading, always thinking, always figuring things out… Now, there are others in the family, but for the purpose of the story, we'll stick with Amnon, Tamar, Absalom, and Solomon. A typical day at the royal court of King David might look something like this.

Solomon: Did you know that the pyramids in Egypt weren't built by slaves but by paid laborers, most likely farmers who needed to earn some extra income while their land was being flooded by the Nile?

Absalom: [a bit bored of him] No, Solomon, I didn't know that.

Solomon: Ask me a question. I bet you I know the answer. Go ahead, ask me.

Absalom: No.

Solomon: [whining] Come on.

Tamar: All right, Solomon. Imagine two countries are at war. How can you end the war without either side losing?

Solomon: Absalom, ask me a question.

Absalom: All right Uh… Two woman have babies. One of the babies dies, and the mother switches it with the other baby. But the other mother figures it out, and says, "My baby's alive, it's yours that's dead." But the first mother says, "No, your baby died.

Mine is still alive." How do you decide who the real mother is and who gets to keep the baby?

[Solomon thinks it over.]

Solomon: First you get a sword and you cut the baby in half.

Tamar: That's disgusting!

Solomon: You probably don't *really* have to cut it in half. Just say you're going to. And then the real mother will be the one who tries to stop you.

Tamar: *I'd* try to stop you! What about trying to convince the women that it's a baby, not a toy to fight over, and get them to share the duties of raising it.

Solomon: You have no sense of logic.

[Amnon is watching Tamar from a distance.]

Amnon: Look at her. [to audience] You hear the voices too, don't you? Telling you to do things, and you're not sure why? They tell me to look at my stepsister Tamar. Just look at the way she moves, the way she dresses, the way she looks at me. The voices tell me I have to have her. I know it's wrong, but the voices don't care. You can't legislate love… But this isn't love… The voices don't care.

[Solomon goes up to Amnon. Tamar and Absalom exit.]

Solomon: Go ahead, Amnon. Ask me a question.

Amnon: [in a whisper] OK, Solomon. Suppose that a man really, *really* wanted his stepsister. Just suppose. And he couldn't find a way to get her alone. What could he do?

Solomon: That's sick.

Amnon: It's just a hypothetical question.

Solomon: Oh, well, *hypothetically*, what he could do is pretend to be really ill, like a stomach flu or some sort of bacterial infection, because then no one will want to be around him. And then he should ask their father to send the stepsister to his room to feed him some chicken soup or something, because he's sick, you see.

Amnon: Right. I see.

Solomon: So, after that…

Amnon: That's fine. I can figure out the rest on my own. You're a smart kid, Solomon.

[Solomon exits. Music. Amnon climbs into "bed," pulling a bedsheet over himself. Tamar enters.]

Tamar: I hear you're not feeling well, brother. I made some soup for you.

[Amnon smiles. Tamar gives Amnon the soup.]

Tamar: There you go.

Amnon: Why don't you have a seat? Stay awhile. We haven't talked in ages.

Tamar: [growing uncomfortable] I should be going.

Amnon: Please.

Tamar: Maybe later.

[Amnon drops the bowl and grabs her.]

Amnon: I insist.

Tamar: Amnon, what are you doing?

[Amnon does not let go.]

Tamar: [forcefully] Amnon, no! Stop it… I'm serious. This isn't funny. Now let go.

Amnon: I'm sick for you.

Tamar: You don't want to do this, Amnon. This isn't how people do things.

Amnon: Rules are meant to be broken.

Tamar: But people aren't. Now stop it, please.

[Tamar tries to leave. Amnon catches her around the waist with the bedsheet. They start a slow dance as Tamar tries to get away and Amnon tries to pull her closer with the sheet.]

Amnon: I've seen the way you look at me.

Tamar: We should talk about this. Let's go to our father and discuss this.

Amnon: Sister! Stop talking.

[The "dance" ends with the bedsheet being slowly ripped in two. Amnon looks at Tamar with disgust, and leaves. Tamar sinks to the floor. She gathers the bedsheet up in a ball and hugs it. Pause. David is still sitting on top of the ladder, in troubled thought.]

Storyteller: David.

David: [not looking] What.

Storyteller: Do you know what's happened?

David: I know.

Storyteller: Well, what are you going to do about it?

[Pause. David does not respond. Absalom enters.]

Absalom: Tamar, my God! What happened to you?

[Pause. They look at each other.]

Absalom: Don't worry. Forget it ever happened. I'll look after everything.

[Absalom exits.]

Storyteller: [to David] Well?

David: Well what?

Storyteller: What are you going to do?

[No response. Tamar, distraught, starts to exit. She stops.]

Tamar: Where am I going? [to audience] I don't want my brother to "look after everything." I don't want to forget it ever happened. How can I? I'm hurt. I feel violated. My stepbrother Amnon… [She can't finish the sentence.] I know what Absalom's going to do, but that's not what I want. That won't help anything or make it better. I don't need…justice. At least not that kind of justice. I need something else. [to David] Daddy? What are you going to do?

[David does not respond. Tamar turns and leaves. Absalom enters.]

Absalom: [to David, angrily] Father! A crime has been committed. Our family honor has been disgraced. What are you going to do?

[David does not respond. Absalom, frustrated, storms out.]

Storyteller: [to David] Is that it? Are you just going to sit there?

David: What do you want me to do?

Storyteller: Don't you think you should do *something*?

[Pause.]

David: My daughter has been…

Storyteller: Raped.

David: Raped.

Storyteller: By…

David: [painfully] By my own son, my heir.

Storyteller: And that's not right.

David: She's being punished for her sins.

Storyteller: She did nothing to deserve that.

David: She's being punished for *my* sins.

Storyteller: Oh, grow up.

David: I was a bad father. I didn't raise my children right. I should have taught him proper values. Instead I let him learn by imitation. And what did he see? A father who takes what he wants, a father who breaks the rules.

Storyteller: [frustrated] David, this isn't about you. It's about Tamar.

David: [angry] Why can't it be about me? I should have been there, but I wasn't. I couldn't stop it from happening. So what do I do now? I can't do anything! It's too late. All I can do is stand on the sidelines and watch. I feel like a bystander at a fatal accident and I hate it!

Storyteller: Just because it's already happened doesn't mean you can't do anything. Your children need you.

David: I don't want to do anything.

Storyteller: I can *see* that. But this demands a response.

David: If I respond to it, then I need to acknowledge the fact that my son has committed a crime. And then what do I do? I'm the king. Do I have my own son arrested? Punished? Executed? I can't do that. And what good will it do? Will it make everything better? No. Then what do I do? Please, just tell me what will make everything better.

Storyteller: I can't.

David: Then I won't do anything.

Storyteller: You can't just ignore it.

David: Things were easier when I was in exile. I knew what was what then. It was exciting, and dangerous, and I loved it. Every choice was life or death and I could take my chances. And I always won. But this…this is too complicated. It's too messy. I don't know what the right thing to do is.

Storyteller: I'm not saying it's easy. But if you don't do anything, you're sending a signal that this is acceptable.

David: Just tell me what to do. All right? Just give a book of rules that will tell me what I'm supposed to do. Something clear. Something in black and white.

Storyteller: Life's not like that.

David: I want it to be.

Storyteller: What happened to the boy who changed the rules, the one who looked for the creative solution?

David: That kid was the underdog. He could laugh it all off; he wasn't in power.

Storyteller: Well, I'm sorry, David, but the kid's a king now. A king and a father. And if you don't do something soon…

> [Amnon and Absalom enter, walking toward each other. David and the Storyteller watch. Absalom is carrying a sword.]

Absalom: [friendly] Amnon!

Amnon: Good day, Absalom.

Absalom: How are you today?

Amnon: Not bad.

Absalom: Good.

> [Absalom kills Amnon.]

Amnon: Aaagh!

Absalom: That's for what you did to my sister.

> [Absalom leaves. Pause. David and the Storyteller stare at Amnon's body.]

David: Things are getting worse.

Storyteller: You have to step in. You can't be an observer anymore.

David: What do I do with this? One of my sons has killed another of my sons. Did Amnon deserve it? Does it matter? Did Absalom have the right…? I hate this. I wish I just knew what the right thing to do was.

> [David looks at the Storyteller for guidance.]

Storyteller: Don't look at me. I'm not even a character at the moment. I'm just narrating.

David: [realizing] Then you can tell me how the story ends.

Storyteller: I can't do that.

David: Then I would know what to do.

Storyteller: I'm not allowed to give that kind of information to a character.

David: Why not?

Storyteller: It's just a rule for storytellers.

David: Then how am I supposed to figure out what to do?!?

Storyteller: Use your heart. Use your head. Do the best you can.

David: What if it's not enough? I have a daughter who's been raped, a son who's been killed, and another son who's a murderer. What if I make things worse?

Storyteller: There's no rule book.

David: Should I punish Absalom, or praise him, or cover the whole thing up and hope that everyone forgets it? Whatever I decide there's going to be someone who says…

[David is cut off by Joab's entrance.]

Joab: King David!

David: Joab.

Joab: Sir, I know this has been a very trying time for you, but things are beginning to get out of hand. Your son Absalom has taken matters into his own hands, and his actions reflect badly on the proper authorities. This sort of vigilante justice is not in the best interest of the crown. It makes you look bad, and it makes *me* look bad. So I'll put it to you plainly, sir, either you do something about it, or I will.

[David looks to the Storyteller. The Storyteller indicates that she is not allowed to tell him anything. David grudgingly acts.]

David: [calling] Absalom!

[Absalom enters.]

David: Absalom.

Absalom: Yes, father.

David: We have a problem.

Absalom: I killed Amnon.

David: You shouldn't have done that.

Absalom: You know what he did to Tamar!

David: Even still, you shouldn't have done that.

Absalom: Why not? He was a criminal, and I was defending our family honor!

David: Even still…

Absalom: You're on his side! I knew you were. You don't care about Tamar at all.

David: That's not true.

Absalom: Oh yeah? Where is she? What have you done to help her? What have you done to make sure this sort of thing doesn't happen again?

David: There are laws…

Absalom: Yeah, and they worked so well *this* time.

David: Absalom! I'm still your father and your king!

Absalom: You're my father and I can't change that, but as for king…

Joab: [threatening] All right, enough of that!

David: Absalom, what you did was wrong. By law I could have you thrown in prison, or executed, but I don't want to do that. So I'm sending you away. You must go into exile. Get out and don't come back.

Absalom: [bitterly] Fine!

[Absalom storms out.]

David: Absalom!

[Absalom does not respond. David is sad.]

David: [to Joab] There, are you happy?

Joab: You might recall another young man who went into exile, later to seize the throne from King Saul. Absalom is disgruntled and has little faith in the current establishment – that is to say, you. He's also quite popular with the people. The proper strategy would have been to keep a man like that close by, so you can keep your eye on him in case he tries to organize a rebellion.

David: Call him back.

[Joab leaves.]

David: [to Storyteller] I hate this.

Storyteller: I know.

David: I had more fun as an outlaw.

[Joab returns.]

Joab: Too late, sir. The rebellion has already started. Absalom is marching toward the city with an army.

David: Is he going to attack the palace?

Joab: It certainly looks that way.

David: Can we hold him off?

Joab: Not very easily.

David: So what do we do?

Joab: I would suggest that we retreat. Vacate the palace and head for the hills. Lay low until things cool down, and then counterattack.

David: You mean, I'm going back into exile?

Joab: That would be my suggestion.

David: Hiding out? Running for my life?

Joab: I'm afraid so.

[David jumps down from the ladder, jubilantly.]

David: Yes!

[David rushes off. Joab follows.]

Storyteller: [to audience] So David went into exile, where decisions were much simpler. Meanwhile Joab worked at regaining control for David. Things were finally decided at the Forest of Ephraim.

[Battle music and sounds of battle.]

Storyteller: Absalom's army was defeated and Absalom himself had to run for his life.

[Absalom runs in.]

Storyteller: Running through the thick forest he got his long hair caught in the branches of an old gnarled oak.

[Absalom runs under the ladder, and gets caught, hanging under the ladder.]

Storyteller: So when David's soldiers found him, he was hanging from a tree, suspended by his hair.

[Two soldiers enter and find Absalom hanging.]

Soldier 1: [not knowing what else to say] Freeze?

Absalom: I'm stuck. Help me down.

Storyteller: Now David had given his men an order before they went to battle…

David: [off to the side] I may regret this, but, if you capture Absalom, deal gently with him. He's still my son. Don't harm him, just bring him home. That's an order.

[Joab enters.]

Joab: What's going on?

Soldier 2: We've found Absalom, sir.

Joab: Fine. Kill him.

Soldier 1: I…don't think we're supposed to do that, sir.

Soldier 2: The king gave us an order. [to Soldier 1] Don't you remember that?

Joab: I'm giving you an order. Now kill him.

[Pause. Joab takes one of the soldiers' spears and kills Absalom, then exits. The soldiers pull Absalom's body down and carry him off. David enters, depressed. He climbs the ladder and sits at the top.]

Storyteller: [to David] David?

David: Go away.

Storyteller: I'm sorry about Absalom.

[David doesn't respond. Joab enters.]

Joab: Sir.

David: Go away, Joab.

Joab: Sir. With all due respect…you're pissing me off. You've won the war. The rebellion has been put down. You should be celebrating, not locking yourself in your room like some sulky child! We lost a lot of good soldiers winning this war for you. But all you care about is the death of one man.

David: He was my son.

Joab: And your enemy. Eggs get broken, David. Lives get lost, and you do what needs to be done. So for God's sake, pull yourself together and be a king. Do the right thing. Thank your people for the work they've done, and be grateful for how good you've got it…sir!

[Joab leaves.]

David: I hate this.

Storyteller: [to audience] And that's the end of that part of the story.

[Music.]

SCENE 5: THE DREAMER

[Music. The Storyteller puts on the cloak of the witch at Endor. David enters, somewhat shyly.]

David: Excuse me.

Witch: Enter stranger. State your need.

David: I was told I might find the woman they call the Witch of Endor here.

Witch: That is a name I carry.

David: I understand you saw King Saul before he died.

Witch: Saul died a long time ago.

David: But are you that same witch of Endor?

Witch: I am.

David: I understand you're very wise.

Witch: I know a cup of water from a clod of dirt. I know a woven cloth from a broken skull. And I know a shepherd from a king.

David: I'm David.

Witch: I see that. What would you have from me?

David: Do you understand dreams?

Witch: Some dreams.

David: I've had a dream that bothers me. It's... You look very familiar. Do I know you?

Witch: I don't know. Do you?

David: I guess not. Anyway, in my dream...

[David "sees" his dream as he describes it.]

David: I am an old man. I've been king for many years. My palace is well-furnished. My armies have been successful. My empire is strong. But the crown is heavy on my head. I am an old man; my body and my mind are sore. I am dying. So I give my son Solomon the crown, and with it a list of political enemies he would do well to dispense with. Including Joab, who killed my Absalom. I tell Solomon to do whatever needs to be done to keep in power.

[Solomon, now a man, enters. David speaks as an old man.]

Solomon: I was thinking that when I'm king I might commission the building of a big temple. Something to keep the people busy, maybe institute forced labor camps. I'd pump a lot of money into it, and get the economy going. What do you think?

David: Say that God told you to do it. That always works.

Solomon: Right.

David: You're going to be a wise king.

Solomon: Thank you, Father.

David: [handing Solomon the crown] Here you go.

[Solomon freezes. David turns back to the Witch. Solomon exits.]

David: And then I died.

Witch: And...

David: And it frightens me.

Witch: You don't want to die.

David: I don't want to become a petty, vindictive old man, more concerned with staying in power and settling scores than with...anything else.

Witch: That is a dream that need not come true.

David: But I think it will. Over the years I've been becoming less creative, more dogmatic, less willing to take risks, more concerned about appearances and comfort, less alive, more like that old man in the dream. You've got to help me.

Witch: What can I do? You seem to know everything there is to know.

David: I want to know why I'm king! Apparently I'm the Lord's anointed, but what does that mean? Shouldn't I be different? Why isn't the world a better place? What's missing…? Saul was the Lord's anointed, but something went wrong, and God bailed out on him. How does something like that happen?

Witch: Do you think I have those answers?

David: I know that Saul asked you to summon the spirit of Samuel. Samuel is the one who anointed both of us. He will have the answers.

Witch: It is a dangerous thing to talk to the dead.

David: This is important.

Witch: [incanting] Give me a space, an empty space, and a long path from Sheol. And loan me a dead man's voice, for only a moment. Send him down that path and let him speak to us.

> [The spirit of Samuel enters.]

Samuel: [grouchy] What am I, on call here?

David: Samuel.

Samuel: What!?!

David: Samuel, it's David. I need some answers.

Samuel: We all need answers. Get in line.

David: Why did Saul fail as king of Israel?

Samuel: Are you surprised? He wasn't a terribly stable person to start with.

David: Then why did you anoint him?

Samuel: Because God told me to. God said, tomorrow a man will come to your house. Anoint him and make him king. So I anoint him and make him king. I don't make the rules, I just follow…

Witch: Show us.

> [Saul and Saul's servant enter, as if approaching a house. Saul knocks on the "door."]

Samuel: [barking] What, what?

Saul: Excuse me, old man, can you help me? I'm looking for my father's donkeys. They seem to have gotten lost.

Samuel: Come here. Kneel down. What's your name?

Saul: Saul, of the house of Benjamin.

[Samuel anoints him.]

Samuel: Saul of the house of Benjamin, you are now the Lord's anointed.

David: Freeze.

[Samuel, Saul, and the servant freeze. David walks into the scene.]

David: Something's wrong here. Who is this man with Saul?

Samuel: That? I don't know. I suppose it's a servant or something.

David: How did you know that the man you were supposed to anoint was Saul, and not his servant?

Samuel: God wouldn't chose a servant as king of Israel.

David: But how did you know?

Samuel: God wouldn't…

David: What if that's it? What if you anointed the wrong man, and that's why Saul didn't work out… Where is this servant now?

Samuel: He's dead, and resting in Sheol. Where I should be!

[Saul and the servant exit. Samuel starts to leave.]

David: Wait! What did God say when he told you to anoint me?

Samuel: He said, "Go, anoint." So I go, anoint. No "Please, Samuel." No "If it's not too much trouble, Samuel."

David: What did God say, exactly?

Samuel: God said, Go to Jesse's youngest and anoint…

David: Wait. "Jesse's youngest" or "Jesse's youngest *son*"?

Samuel: Jesse's youngest, Jesse's youngest son, whatever. Go and anoint this kid and…

David: No, this is important. Did God say, "Anoint Jesse's youngest"?

Samuel: I don't remember.

David: Because I have a sister. A younger sister. I'm the youngest son, but she's the youngest child. So this is important.

Samuel: Girls don't rule countries. Whatever God said, God *meant* you.

David: But how do you know?

Samuel: Stop asking me that, will you! Are you a prophet? Do you have to deal with God muttering in your ear all day? God mumbles. Do you know that? It's true. My hearing's fine; it's God who mumbles. So I interpret; I fill in the blanks.

David: You make assumptions.

Samuel: I make my best guess.

David: But what if your best guess is wrong?

Samuel: What do I care? I'm dead. Good night.

[Samuel exits.]

David: What if he anointed the wrong person? What if it's not me who is supposed to be ruling, what if it's…

[He looks at and recognizes the witch.]

David: It's you! I knew you looked familiar. You're Han. My sister, Han!

[Hannah, the Storyteller, takes off the cloak.]

Witch/Hannah: I've worn many names, but Hannah was the first.

David: Han!

Hannah: Davie.

David: What are you doing here? How did you get here?

Hannah: I'll tell you the story. When you left with Samuel, I stayed home and played the good daughter. I did everything that was expected of me, and I hated it. So, years later, when you fled from Saul's court and went into exile, I wanted to go and join up with you.

[Jesse enters.]

Jesse: No! No daughter of mine is going off gallivanting with a bunch of rogues and cutthroats.

Han: [to Jesse] But father, it's David.

Jesse: I don't care. It's no place for a girl.

Han: I'm not a girl anymore, father.

Jesse: Whatever. It's not right for a woman to be going off on her own. It isn't safe. It isn't right.

Han: I want to get out. I want to *do* something.

Jesse: Then clean the dishes. That's something.

Han: Father, I'm going into exile to join David.

Jesse: You are not!

Han: I am, and you can't stop me.

Jesse: All right then, go. From this moment on, I have no daughter. You'll get nothing from me. Hannah does not exist.

Han: [furious] Fine!

[Jesse exits.]

Hannah: [to David] So I left home. But once I got out on my own, I realized that all I'd really wanted was to be free. And it didn't make sense to rush from the protection of my father to the protection of my brother. So instead I went out on my own, traveling around, meeting people, getting to know different ways of being and living.

David: By yourself?

Hannah: For a time. Eventually I met some other women who, like me, for whatever reasons, didn't have a home. And some of these women were carriers of a wisdom.

[Wise women enter.]

Woman 1: Walk with me, Hannah. I'll teach you my obvious secrets.

Woman 2: Walk with me, Hannah, and I'll tell you of the laws that lie beneath the law, and the rules that cut through the word.

Woman 1: Walk with me, Hannah, and I'll sing you songs. Songs for making and songs for changing, songs for summoning and songs for concealing.

Woman 2: Walk with me, Hannah.

Hannah: [to woman] Why?

Woman 2: For the company.

[The wise women exit.]

Hannah: [to David] So I learned ways of seeing and skills for doing, and eventually I laid claim to this cave and started a fire. Which is when Saul came to me, cloaked in failure and despair… So I gave him soup. And watched him go out to die… Then I heard that you were king, and I was happy for you.

David: Were you?

Hannah: I'm still your little sister, Davie. I'll always be proud of you.

David: [realizing] You came to the palace.

Hannah: True, I wasn't *always* proud of you. When I saw what you had done to Bathsheba and Uriah, I put on the cloak of a man and became for a time a prophet. I changed my name from "Han" to "Not Han," and from there to "Nathan."

[Hannah puts on the Nathan cloak.]

David: "You are that man."

Nathan/Hannah: "Everything is connected." I enjoyed the disguise and the freedom of being a man in the world, but eventually I had to take my name back, and be myself again. [taking the cloak off] So I came back here. And over the years a community has formed around me. Mostly of women, but some men too. People who've been shut out or sent away. People who've had to flee. People without a proper place in the world. After her rape, your daughter Tamar came here to be with me, to grow and heal.

[Tamar enters.]

David: Tamar!

Tamar: Hello, Father.

David: [to Hannah] You were part of the story the whole time.

Hannah: Yes. And living my own story, hidden just behind yours.

David: And you looked after my daughter.

Hannah: She's a strong woman. We've all learned lessons of compassion and wisdom from her.

David: Tamar, I…

Tamar: Did you even notice that I was gone?

[Pause.]

Hannah: Tamar is a musician, like you. Sing that song for your father. [to David] She calls it "Hannah's Song" because I helped her with the words.

[Tamar sings. The rest of the cast enters and may join in.]

Tamar: My soul cries out.

To you, O God, we sing.

Lift up the weak and let them speak

And heal each broken thing.

Break down the walls.

Unlock the chains that bind.

Let all who cling to pow'r and things

Be changed or left behind.

Fill us with strength.

With us your Spirit fill,

To live the laws that give all life,

Resist all laws that kill.

We will not rest.

Our dreaming will not pause,

Until your Rule to break all rules

Is Law to end all laws.

My soul cries out.

To you, O God, we sing.

Lift up the weak and let them speak

And heal each broken thing.

David: [to Hannah] If it had been you and not me, would you have done things differently?

Hannah: Of course.

David: Better?

Hannah: Who's to say?

David: But you couldn't use a sling to save your life. How would you have got past Goliath?

Hannah: Perhaps by not killing him.

[David takes off the crown and offers it to Hannah.]

David: This crown should have been yours. I know it's late, but…

Hannah: Thank you, Davie, but I don't need it. What I've done is as important as being a ruler and a lawmaker. This is my place.

David: I can't go back, Hannah. The power, the laws. It doesn't mean anything to me anymore. I want to part of a revolution again. I want to be part of this…if you'll let me.

Hannah: What about the throne?

Tamar: He needs to be here, Aunt Hannah.

David: I could abdicate to Solomon. He's a smart young man.

Hannah: You also have a daughter.

David: That could be very interesting.

Tamar: You know this isn't how the story goes.

David: What good is a story if you can't change the ending?

[Tamar climbs the ladder and stands near the top. David is welcomed into the group behind Hannah.]

Hannah/Storyteller: [to audience] A story can be a dream, a vision of things to come. This is the story of David, and of Hannah, and Tamar, and Jonathan, and Goliath, and Saul. And the story ends here. But others begin. All stories cross each other at one point or another. Everything is connected. Find your own story. If it doesn't work, change it. Use your imagination to give yourself settings, and characters, and action… Make it in your mind. For what you make in your mind is only a step away from real… Then step.

[The end.]

WORK

SCENE 1: THE INTERVIEWS

[Five empty chairs sit in a row across center stage. Five people enter in a line: Matthew, Shelby, Ian, Sarah, and Gwen. They are all in their mid-20s. They wear white dress shirts, ties, blue jeans, and black Doc Marten shoes. When they get to the chairs they stop and turn to face the audience. Matthew sits, Shelby sits, Ian sits, Sarah sits, Gwen sits.

They sit for a moment, waiting. Matthew checks his watch, Shelby checks her watch, Ian checks his watch, Sarah checks her watch, Gwen checks her watch. Simultaneously they all cross their legs. Someone starts to tap his foot. Others tap their feet, impatiently. The various tappings meld into a common rhythm.

Throughout this section each actor will step forward and speak to the audience as if speaking to a job interviewer. As each character speaks, the others will tap their feet in a rhythm appropriate to the character.

Matthew rises and steps forward. He is a shy, nervous young man. We hear both the words he is saying to the interviewer and the words he is thinking in his head.]

Matthew: (I am a talented and capable person. I am a talented and capable person. I am a talented, and capable, person...)

Hi. I'm Matthew.

Uh, social insurance number 654 386 221.

Hi. Hi. Hi...

Oh, um, well, what can I tell you, um... As you can see from my resumé, I graduated from university last year with very high marks, and...

Sorry?

Of Manitoba, yes.

What have I been doing for the past year?

Well, um, mostly looking for work in my field of expertise. Well, not *expertise*, per se, but my field of interest. I mean, not just interest, but...

Why do, do I think I'm the best, best person for this job?

Um, um, well, let me see. I'm...smart? I'm, a fast learner. I'm familiar with Macintosh, IBM, Windows, Microsoft Office, Photoshop, Netscape, Mosaic, and Quicken. Um, um, um... When I was in high school my classmates voted me "Most Likely to Succeed," and they gave me a briefcase. Of course, no one ever actually told me the *combination* to the briefcase, so I haven't actually used it all that much. I suppose I could have asked somebody, but…

(Oh God, I'm lost. What am I talking about? I don't even remember what the question was. Why am I the best person for the job? They're interviewing 4000 people, 4000 people, and I'm supposed to convince them I'm the best?!)

Can I just say that, that, if you hire me, I think I could do an excellent job, I mean, a really good, really pretty very good…job. Thank you.

(OK, here it comes, here it comes. The rejection. Oh God, oh God, they hate me. They hate me and they're going to tell all their friends. OK, OK, here we go…)

I understand. I understand.

Well, thank you for your time, and, and if anything else ever comes up…?

I understand. Thank you.

> [Matthew sheepishly returns to his seat. Shelby bounds forward. She is enthusiastic to the extreme.]

Shelby: Hi there, my name's Shelby. My social insurance number is 673 843 021, and I think I'm the person you're looking for. I'm a natural communicator, I'm outgoing, I'm friendly, I love working with people. I'm an extrovert by nature. I speak English, French, a little bit of Spanish, a little bit of Ukrainian…

No, I don't have a masters' degree in communications, but…

Yes, and that makes perfect sense, but, you see, here's the thing… The requirements for graduate school are pretty strict. The only people they're accepting into the communications program are people with at least two years of practical experience in the field. Which is why I'd really like to get this job, you see. So I can get the work experience necessary to get into the communications program, so I can get the master's degree, so that I can apply for the positions that require it… Like this one. Did I mention that I own my own car?

> [Shelby returns to her seat. Ian steps forward. His humor covers a bitterness.]

Ian: Ian. Number 649 537 812.

My idea of a perfect job…? Hmm. Well, a couple of years ago the government decided to play around with U.I. They put a bunch of restrictions on who could get it and who couldn't, and they changed the name from Unemployment Insurance to *Employment* Insurance. Employment sounds better, doesn't it? Everyone likes employment. The only problem is that when you change the name of a government program you also have to change all the forms and documents related to it. Forms, documents, manuals, anything anywhere that says "Unemployment Insurance" goes to the shredder, and then it's off to Dave's Quick Prints to get new ones. So I'm thinking, working at Dave's Quick Prints would be a pretty good job. Better yet, the government could hire me and a bunch of my friends, give us eight dollars an hour and a big ol' bottle of White Out, and we'll go through every document by hand, whiting out the "un's". For an extra dollar an hour, we could even white-out the "un's" in unthinking, unaware, unfathomable, and unpopular.

> [Ian returns to his seat. All the actors stand simultaneously, circle their chair clockwise, and sit again. Gwen steps forward. She is pragmatic and strong.]

Gwen: My name is Gwen, my SIN number is 639 475 338.

I'll be honest with you. I'm here because I need this job. I have a four-year-old daughter to support. I've done welfare, and I don't want to do it anymore.

No, no, I believe in welfare, and it's not that I'm too proud. I've just found that welfare is too unreliable. It's always a hassle, and they treat you like dirt. Now I realize I'm probably not as qualified as some of the other people you've got applying, but if you give me this job I'll work hard and you'll be able to count on me. I like to be direct, and I don't play games so... Do I have any kind of chance at this job...?

Thank you for being straightforward. I appreciate that.

> [Gwen sits back down. Shelby rushes forward again.]

Shelby: Hi there. Shelby, 673 843 021.

I love research, I love books...

No, I love working on my own. In fact, in some ways, I prefer it. I'm an introvert by nature. I can go weeks without talking to another human being. I'm meticulous, and thorough, and just really a very quiet, steady worker. And it's always been a dream of mine to be an archivist...

Did I mention I own my own car?

> [Shelby sits. Sarah steps forward. She is thoughtful and sincere, and tries to answer each question as honestly and as thoroughly as she can.]

Sarah: Hello. My name is Sarah. My social insurance number is 675 299 314, I believe....

Why do I think I deserve this job?

I'm not entirely sure I do. I have no doubt that I would be good at it. I think I have the skills and the experience it requires. But to say that I *deserve* this job given the number of people in this country who are unemployed, given that some parts of the country are at 40, 50, *90* percent unemployment, I'm thinking especially of some of the aboriginal communities not to mention the whole two-thirds world... To say, in that context, that I *deserve* this job... I mean, how could I say that I am *more* deserving of this job than someone else? On what grounds could I make such a claim? By some inherent moral excellence in my personality? By some crap shoot of genetics, geography, and social location? And wouldn't saying that I deserve this job necessarily imply that all the others *don't* deserve it? That those who are unemployed *don't* deserve jobs? That, in fact, those who are without work *deserve* to be without meaningful work? And again, on what grounds? *Lack* of moral excellence? Random chance, luck of the draw…?

No, I realize you weren't looking for a philosophical analysis. And I would still like the job. I'm just suddenly trying to wrestle with the moral implications of getting it…

Ah, well, thank you for saving me the trouble then.

[Sarah sits. Matthew psyches himself up to step forward again.]

Matthew: (Confidence. Confidence. You are a talented and capable person. All you have to do is let them see that. Be yourself. OK, maybe not *yourself*, per se, but someone very like you, who is talented, and capable, and confident, and calm. Calm… Calm.)

Hello.

Yes, I'm Matthew, 654 386 221.

It's a pleasure to meet you…

I think I'd be very good at this job. I'm confident, I'm capable, I'm talented, I'm flexible, and this is an area of particular interest to me…

What are my weaknesses? What, what, what, what do you mean, what are my weaknesses?

(What are my weaknesses?! What kind of, what kind of question is that? What do they want me to say? That I'm lazy, that I'm a perpetual failure, that I'm deathly afraid of all authority figures? Or do they want me to say that I don't have any weaknesses? But they'd know I was lying for sure. Are they testing my confidence, or are they trying to see if I'm some sort of megalomaniacal psycho? Oh my God, I'm doomed!)

What are my weaknesses? W-W-Why, what have you heard?

[Matthew slinks to the other end of the row. Shelby jumps into Matthew's old chair, Ian into Shelby's, and so on down the row. Matthew takes the seat vacated by Gwen. He will remain there for quite a while, trying to get his nerve up. Shelby steps forward.]

Shelby: My weaknesses? Oh, gosh, that's a hard one. I guess I'd have to say that my greatest weakness is that I work too hard. Sometimes, when a project is coming due, I'll stay up all night for days in a row, just to get it finished. I don't even charge overtime. Just go, go, go. I'm always pushing myself.

Does that make me a workaholic? I don't know. But you know, I never get stressed…

Well, it's kind of always been a dream of mine to work in advertising. I loved that billboard campaign your company did last fall.

Did I mention that I own my own car?

[Shelby down, Gwen up.]

Gwen: Hi there. My name's Gwen.

639 475 338.

I'm wondering whether you have any job openings…?

Anything…

Anything…

Anything…

OK, well can I leave you my resumé? Thanks.

[Gwen starts to leave, sees something out of the corner of her eye, and returns.]

What did you just do with my resume?

Well, give it back. If I'd wanted it thrown out I could have done it myself.

[Gwen down, Ian up.]

Ian: 649 537 812.

Yes, I realize it looks like I haven't been doing anything for the last four years, but I've been working. I just haven't been paid…

For the government. Kind of a civil service job. You see, the current economic theory is that low unemployment leads to high inflation, so, the way I see it, by not being able to get a job for the last four years I've been protecting the Canadian people from high interest rates and the ravages of inflation…

That's OK, you don't have to thank me. Your heartfelt indifference is thanks enough.

[Ian sits. Matthew steps forward but immediately chickens out and sits again. Shelby rushes forward.]

Shelby: Hobbies? Well, I like all sorts of things. I play racquetball and tennis. I really enjoy going to movies and the theater. I love to read, and I've been thinking about getting into –

[Shelby sees something in the interviewer's expression that causes her to slam on the brakes and make a sudden shift in strategy.]

But I've been trying to cut back on all of those things because I'd really like to focus on work. No distractions. Nothing to keep me from devoting 110 percent of my energy to work. I don't have a family. No boyfriend. I don't even really have any friends. Just work. Work is what will give my life meaning. I mean, who needs a life when you've got work, right?

[Shelby back to her seat, Gwen forward.]

Gwen: 639 475 338.

My life? Well… I have a daughter, who's beautiful, and some friends, but I've sort of given up on the idea of life in favor of survival. It's all part of a process of lowering my expectations. I figure if I get my expectations low enough I might actually be pleasantly surprised by something someday…

No, I wouldn't describe myself as an angry person. Just envious.

[Gwen down, Sarah up.]

Sarah: Sarah, 675 299 314…

Retail? No, I don't have much in the way of retail experience. The closest I've come, I suppose, is selling chocolates in junior high to fund a band trip. Of course, my parents bought all of them, but…

Well, I think I could be a capable salesperson…

What do I think I'd be selling? I would assume that since this is a *sporting goods* store that I'd be selling sporting goods…

I'll be selling myself…? I'm, I'm not sure I understand…

Ah, I see. I'm not just selling sporting goods, I'm selling myself… So that would make you not so much my *boss* as my pimp…? That was just a little joke…

I understand.

[Sarah sheepishly returns to her seat. Shelby rushes forward, still bursting with manic enthusiasm and a willingness to say whatever it takes.]

Shelby: Shelby, 673 843 021…

I love shoes! I wear shoes! I think that makes me something of an expert!

It's sort of always been a dream of mine to work in a discount shoe store!

[Shelby down, Sarah up.]

Sarah: My weaknesses? I think, I think too much. I ask questions that shouldn't be asked…

Like what? Like what's the real work of people in our society? I mean, we do all sorts of jobs, but the real occupation of our culture seems to be consumption. I know this is true, because whenever I think of all the things I'll never own I feel scared. Our economy is based on a large army of professional consumers. Every day we bite off huge chunks of the earth, chew it up, and spit it out. And all our other work is just to support that. Every year we have to produce more, faster, cheaper, with fewer workers, and every year our consumption has to increase just to keep the ball rolling. So, I have to ask, how long can a system like that be sustained? But that's not a question you ask in this culture. Because if you ask, you don't eat.

[Sarah sits, Ian rises.]

Ian: 649 537 812.

I don't want to get all conspiracy theory here, but I've got this sneaking suspicion we were raised to be sacrificial lambs. I mean, why else would our elementary school teachers teach us all those *cooperative* games and tell us we could be anything we wanted in the world? By the time there are any openings in the job market, we'll have racked up 15, 20 years of bitterness and inactivity… My generation was born under a mushroom cloud of nuclear fatalism. A lot of us never expected to reach adulthood… Now that I'm here, I hate to admit it, but I'm a little bit disappointed.

[Ian returns to his seat. During this last speech, Matthew has started to drift off. Shelby stomps her feet, followed by Ian, followed by Sarah, followed by Gwen. When it gets to the end of the row, Matthew is startled and falls off his chair. The other four look at him and roll their eyes. Sarah, Ian, and Shelby turn away from him. Gwen helps him back onto his chair. The other three turn forward again as Shelby rises and steps forward.]

Shelby: Shelby, 673 843 021…

My education? Well, let me see. I've got a bachelor of arts in medieval literature and communication studies, a certificate in multimedia computer programming, a certificate in introductory business management, a diploma in chartered accountancy, a couple of courses in veterinary medicine, a continuing education course in auto mechanics, life guard training, Saint John's Ambulance first aid, screenplay writing, journalism, therapeutic message, and raku pottery…

Overeducated?! No! I haven't retained anything from these courses! I'm a blank slate! I'm a blank slate!

[An anxious Shelby returns to her seat as a tired Gwen steps forward.]

Gwen: Gwen, 639 475 338…

639 475 338…

639 475 338…

What do you mean my employment insurance has run out…?

But don't you have to send out a letter or something? Even something saying, "This is your last check"? I mean, what am I supposed to do now…?

How is that *not* your problem?!

Forget it.

Forget it!

> [Gwen returns to her seat, shaking her head in frustration. Shelby rushes forward, still smiling desperately.]

Shelby: Shelby, 673 843 021!

Hi there! Let me just say, it's sort of always been a dream of mine to work in a music store…

Because I love music. Music is life…

All kinds of music. Rock, pop, country, jazz, folk, classical…

Where do I see myself in five years? …Here. Working here. In this music store. For ten cents more than minimum wage.

> [Matthew gears himself up for one more interview.]

Matthew: (OK, Matthew, this is it. This is the one. All those other people are idiots compared to you. You are the next stage of human evolution. You are the answer to all their dreams. You are their messiah. Accept no opposition. Don't see the job, *be* the job. Eye of the tiger, eye of the tiger. OK, here goes…)

Hello!

Matthew!

Number 654 386 221!

Because I'm the man to do this job!

I have all the skills you need and some you haven't even imagined yet…

Where do I see myself in five years? I see myself well on my way up the corporate ladder. I see myself as the CEO! I see myself running this company and firing your sorry baby-boomer asses, and replacing you with a team of over-educated slackers who've been forced to flip burgers and serve *cafe lattes* for the past eight years. I see myself running this corporation like my own private fiefdom and using it as a jumping-off place to world domination!

> [Pause. Matthew realizes he has gone too far.]

OK, um, here's the thing. I'm, I'm, I'm white, I'm straight, I'm male, and I'm middle class. I understand that society is supposed to give people like me all sorts of unearned privileges, and I was wondering if I could, you know, maybe, cash some of those in now?

> [Matthew goes back to the row as Shelby steps forward. Shelby speaks to the audience directly, not to an interviewer. The others kneel in front of their chairs.]

Shelby: Every morning, before I get out of bed, I say this prayer: O holy and transcendent job market, blessed be thy name. Look favorably upon me today. Let your face shine upon me, and let me be what you are looking for. Thy kingdom come, thy will be done, in Winnipeg as it is in Toronto, as it is in New York, as it is in the Philippines. Give me today some daily bread, and maybe a little something to put in my RRSP so I don't starve to death when I'm old. And I wouldn't say no to some dental insurance either. And lead me not into dead-end jobs, but deliver me from my student loan. For thine is the kingdom and the power and the glory, forever and ever, amen.

[And then everyone back on their chairs.]

SCENE 2: THE WAITING GAME

[A simultaneous stomp. All wait expectantly for the phone to ring. The foot tapping rhythm continues.

The phone rings. Gwen runs to get it. Sarah grabs her hand, pulls her back, and runs for the phone herself. By the time she gets there, Shelby has already arrived and answered the phone. Sarah stands, impatiently staring at Shelby.]

Shelby: Hello...?

Oh, hi.

Look, I can't talk. I took a bunch of resumés around last week and I'm waiting for a call. I'll phone you tonight.

[All return to their seats. More waiting. The phone rings again. Gwen runs for it. Sarah pulls her back, and runs for it. Gwen grabs Sarah's hand and spins her around to the back of the row of chairs. Gwen runs for the phone and answers it.]

Gwen: Hello...?

OK, well, thanks anyway.

[Gwen returns to her seat. The phone rings again. Matthew runs for it, but is pulled back by Gwen, who runs for it, but is pulled back by Sarah, who runs for it, but is pulled back by Ian, who runs for it, but is pulled back by Shelby. Shelby rushes to the phone and answers it.]

Shelby: Hello...?

Yes.

Yes.

YES!! All right! That's great!

Sorry...?

Oh.

No, that's fine. That's great. It's like a, like a five-day weekend, every week. It's great. I couldn't have arranged it better myself. Thanks.

[Shelby returns to her seat.]

SCENE 3: WORK MAKES FREE

[A simultaneous stomp.]

All: Work!

[Gwen steps forward. The others rise and put their hands on their hips, as managers.]

All: Give me a "W"!

Gwen: W!

All: Give me an "A"!

Gwen: A!

All: Give me an "L"!

Gwen: L!

All: Give me a squiggle!

[Pause. Gwen winces.]

All: Give me a squiggle!

Gwen: Do I have to?

All: Yes. Give me a squiggle!

Gwen: Squiggle.

[Gwen swallows her pride and squiggles her bum to the floor.]

All: Give me a "Mart"!

Gwen: Mart.

All: What do you get?

Gwen: Wal-Mart.

All: What's that again?

Gwen: Wal-Mart.

All: Who's number one?

Gwen: [half-heartedly] The customer. Always. Ka-ching.

> [Gwen returns to her chair and stands in front of it. Matthew sits and mimes speaking on the phone. Gwen stands and mimes speaking into a check-out microphone. Sarah stands and mimes moving things along a conveyer belt. Ian stands and mimes flipping hamburger patties. Shelby stands and mimes pulling shoeboxes down from a shelf and trying shoes on someone's foot.]

Ian: Order up!

Gwen: Price check.

Shelby: Size nine.

Ian: Fries with that?

Sarah: Next, please.

Matthew: I'm calling on behalf of...

All: Have a nice day!

> [Stomp. The actions and the phrases repeat, getting faster and faster, becoming more sing-songy. After a few repetitions at this tempo, the characters get tired and bored and the rhythm starts to slow down. The actors stop their actions. The words become more monotone. Until...]

Ian: Order up.

Gwen: Price check.

Shelby: Size nine.

Ian: *My soul* with that?

Sarah: Next, please.

Matthew: I'm calling on behalf of...

All: Have a nice day.

> [Stomp. They stop, exhausted.
>
> All the standing actors (i.e., not Matthew) take a deep breath and then march to the front of the stage. In a row across the front of the stage they march quickly in place.

Once the marching rhythm is established, Sarah trips and falls out of line. Matthew rushes to fill in her space. Then Ian stumbles and falls, and Sarah jumps in to fill his space. Ian steps off to the side and addresses the audience.]

Ian: An expendable worker is a busy worker. Remember: There are thousands of people out there just waiting to replace you.

[Shelby stumbles out of the marching line, and Ian jumps into her place. Shelby tries to join on at the end of the line, but Ian pushes her away. Gwen stumbles out, and Shelby rushes into her space. Gwen waits a moment for someone to stumble out, but when no one does, she takes matters into her own hands. She grabs Matthew and pulls him out of the line, taking his place. Matthew grabs Sarah and pulls her out, taking her place. Sarah goes off to the side of the stage and sits, dejected.

The marching speeds up a notch. Ian stumbles out. Shelby, Gwen, and Matthew freeze. Angry and frustrated Ian walks to the back of the stage, knocking over a chair as he passes.

There are now only three actors at center stage – Shelby, Gwen, and Matthew. The marching resumes, but faster. Eventually Matthew stumbles out. Shelby and Gwen freeze. Matthew slinks back to the row of chairs and crouches behind a chair.

The marching resumes, but very quickly now. Shelby and Gwen are both trying to keep up with each other. There is a bit of jostling between them. Finally Gwen trips and stumbles out. Shelby keeps marching. Gwen, frustrated and despairing, starts to leave the stage, but, realizing that she can't afford to, returns to the row of chairs and sits.

Shelby is now alone at center stage, marching at breakneck speed, almost running on the spot. She is showing signs of exhaustion. Finally the strain of maintaining that pace becomes too great, and she collapses.

Sarah rises and addresses the audience. As she speaks, Ian, Gwen, and Matthew gather around Shelby, and help her up.]

Sarah: When some have no work and some have too much, when some work for 60 hours a week and some for only ten, when all the really important work of the world gets left undone because no one's willing to pay for it, then there's something seriously wrong with this picture… Something in this system simply doesn't work. Something in this system simply doesn't work… For God's sake, imagine something new.

[All the actors walk off in different directions. As they pass the row of chairs they each grab a chair and move it slightly. The actors leave the stage. What was once a row of chairs is now more of an open ended circle. The end.]

JUST 'CAUSE

[A full-length mirror. A coat tree, with a pair of jeans and a leather jacket hanging. A wooden chair. A bride. White dress, veil, bouquet. The dress should come in two parts – a bodice-type top and a poofy tulle skirt. Underneath the dress the bride should wear a tank top and either shorts or tights.

The bride takes a breath, and smiles. The theme from Mendelssohn's *Wedding March* plays. She doesn't move. Pause.]

Bride: Yes… This is the happiest day of my life. I'm wearing my mother's wedding gown. The church is perfectly decorated. The inventory list from the bridal magazine is a series of checkmarks. Everything is perfect.

[Pause. She doesn't move. The theme from Mendelssohn's *Wedding March* plays again. She still doesn't move. Still smiling.]

Bride: The beginning of a new life together. A new family. A family of my own. Everything is perfect.

[Pause. She doesn't move. She just smiles. Her mom creeps in and approaches her, cautiously, so as not to frighten or upset her.]

Mom: Honey?

[The bride keeps staring straight ahead. Smiling.]

Bride: Hi, Mom.

Mom: How are you doing?

Bride: Just fine, Mom. Everything's perfect.

Mom: That's great, honey. Are you ready to get started?

Bride: On my new life?

Mom: …Yes, dear.

Bride: My new family?

Mom: That's right, dear.

Bride: Yes.

[Long pause. The bride stares straight ahead, smiling. The mom stands to the side, waiting. Finally…]

Bride: Hell.

[The bride tosses the bouquet to the floor, throws the veil on the chair, and starts fumbling with the buttons on the bodice.]

Mom: Honey?

Bride: What am I doing? Who needs this? Who are we doing this for? I don't need a new life. I have a life! A good one.

Mom: Jane?

Bride: How did I let myself get sucked into this! I don't need an expensive party. I don't need a ceremony, or a ritual, or a legal document to validate my relationship. I *know* it's valid.

[She pulls off the bodice and throws it on the chair. She starts climbing out of the skirt.]

Mom: Now, dear…

Bride: I thought, "It's no big deal. Just a little ritual, just a legal contract. It doesn't define me. I'm still the same person. Saying 'I do' isn't going to instantaneously transform me into some sort of Donna Reed/June Cleaver pre-feminist automaton!" But it's the first compromise, isn't it? The first allowance to a system of institutionalized relationship that discourages diversity by rewarding superficial conformity, and with each allowance it becomes harder and harder to do anything unique, revolutionary, or authentic! Why would I want to artificially legitimize my relationship by forcing it into a pre-existing cookie-cutter template?

Mom: All right, dear, I have no idea what you just said, but…

Bride: I'm not getting married.

[She jumps out of the skirt.]

Bride: That's so much better! Now I can breathe again.

[Slight pause.]

Mom: All right now, Janie, you're having a little panic attack. This is just cold feet; it happens all the time.

Bride: It's not cold feet, Mom. It's an epiphany!

Mom: …An epiphany.

Bride: Right. Everything suddenly makes sense.

Mom: I see. You're rethinking all your previous assumptions?

Bride: Exactly!

Mom: You're starting to see your actions in a larger context?

Bride: That's it!

Mom: Honey, that's the *definition* of a panic attack. Now let's get you dressed, so…

Bride: No, Mom, I'm serious. I have this strong intuition that if I walk into that ceremony, and I get married to Mark, I will be committing a terrible, terrible injustice.

Mom: Honey, don't exaggerate. This is the happiest day of your entire life! …Have you found out something about Mark that you're not telling me?

Bride: I don't think so.

Mom: You've just decided you don't love him.

Bride: Oh, no, I still love him. I just don't want to marry him.

Mom: …You love him.

Bride: Right.

Mom: …But you don't want to marry him.

Bride: No.

Mom: Why on earth not?

Bride: …I'm not quite sure.

Mom: Well then…

[Mom starts to get the bride dressed again, starting with the skirt.]

Bride: No, wait! I do know why. Because it would feel like I was collaborating to further entrench an already firmly entrenched system of oppression.

[Slight pause.]

Mom: So, this is purely ideological.

Bride: Hmm. I guess so.

Mom: Honey, nobody cancels a wedding at the last minute for ideological reasons.

Bride: They don't?

[Mom continues dressing the bride again, doing up the skirt and then adding the veil.]

Mom: No, they don't. And more importantly, there are 200 people in the next room waiting to see you get married. That's what they came for. That's why you invited them. Some of them came from far away just to be here for your special day.

Bride: Oh.

Mom: It would be very rude to disappoint them, wouldn't it?

Bride: I guess so.

[Slight pause. The bride takes the veil off.]

Bride: On the other hand, they *are* my friends and family. They wouldn't want to see me compromise my principles, even if they *had* flown in from Sault Sainte Marie. I could just explain it to them. They'd understand.

[The bride looks to her mom for confirmation. Her mom raises one eyebrow, skeptically.]

Bride: OK, Grandma wouldn't understand. Or Auntie Ruth, but… Or cousin Dan, but… Oh, who am I kidding? You're right. Let's just get this over with.

Mom: That's a good girl.

[Mom gets the bodice from the chair. Meanwhile, the bride has a thought and throws off the veil and starts to climb out of the skirt.]

Bride: Wait a minute! What kind of a cop-out is *that*?!? I should put on this big poofy white thing and walk down the aisle just because it would be socially awkward *not* to?

Mom: I don't understand, Jane. Don't you want to get married?

Bride: No.

Mom: But don't you *want* to get married?

Bride: That's what this is about, Mom.

Mom: I know, but don't you want to get married?

Bride: MOM!

Mom: I just want you to be happy!

Bride: I want to be happy too.

Mom: Don't you want to have children?

Bride: Sure I do.

Mom: Well, how can a person have children if they don't get married?

[Slight pause.]

Bride: Mom…

Mom: Oh god. Oh, don't even, don't even…!

[The bride puts on a pair of jeans and a leather jacket from the coat tree.]

Bride: Look, Mom, I'm still figuring it out myself, but it has something to do with this sudden realization that I already have a family. A pretty all-inclusive family of people I love. Whether I'm married to them, or related by blood, or not. If I choose to have them around me, they're my family.

Mom: Of course, dear. And you've chosen Mark. That's what this wedding is all about. So we can celebrate what a wonderful choice you've made.

Bride: But what if I made a different choice? What if I chose to spend the rest of my life with my friend Sandra?

[Slight pause.]

Mom: Jane, are you coming out of the closet?

Bride: Answer the question first.

Mom: I, I, I don't remember what the question was.

Bride: If I was choosing to spend my life with Sandra instead of Mark, would there be the same celebration? Would friends and relatives come from all over? Would there be books and magazines devoted to the ceremony? Would you be as happy as you are with the idea of Mark?

[Pause.]

Mom: You're my daughter… I love you no matter what. And if you chose someone, they must be pretty great.

[Slight pause.]

Mom: How was that?

Bride: That was pretty good, Mom. And no, I'm not coming out of the closet. My point is that marriage celebrates and legitimizes one kind of relationship, and leaves the rest out in the cold. So if I want to live my life with Mark, great. But if I want to live my life with Sandra, what then? If I want to live my life with my friend Simon, what then?

Mom: Isn't Simon your gay friend?

Bride: He's a friend who happens to be gay, yes.

Mom: Well, dear, unless I've misunderstood the concept of "gay," the idea of you and Simon as a couple…

Bride: There's more to relationships than sex, Mom. Great Aunt Mildred and Ailsa MacDonald have lived together their entire lives, and so far as anyone knows they're not lovers…

Mom: Are you *trying* to start rumors?!

Bride: …But they're still family to each other. I want a definition of family that acknowledges that there might be *other* kinds of relationship.

Mom: But if you love *Mark*, why does that matter?

Bride: Because, someday, when I'm in hospital, on my deathbed, I want my family to be there.

Mom: What? What are you saying? Deathbed?! You're not dying!

Bride: I'm trying to explain. Someday, when I'm in hospital, on my deathbed, I'm going to want the people I love to be with me. And I don't want someone I love to be shut out because they don't fit in to the hospital's definition of family.

Mom: Why are you talking like this? Deathbeds! Dying!

Bride: I'm just saying…

Mom: I don't want to hear this. It's your wedding day! And besides, that wouldn't happen.

Bride: It does happen.

Mom: I can't believe you're talking about dying at a time like this.

Bride: It's an illustration.

Mom: Listen, dear, I'm your mother. It's my job to worry about you. I don't want you to end up sad and alone.

Bride: What makes you think I'm going to end up sad and alone?

Mom: I know it sounds old fashioned, but unless you walk down that aisle, sign on the dotted line, and say "til death do us part," you've got no guarantee. He could up and walk out on a moment's notice.

Bride: But Mom, you and Dad both said "til death do us part," and ten years later you were divorced.

Mom: Is that what this is about? You're afraid that you and Mark are going to end up like your father and me?

Bride: I'm just saying that marriage isn't a guarantee of anything. Half of all marriages end in divorce.

Mom: I knew that it would come back to haunt me.

Bride: Mom, stop it.

Mom: You're afraid of commitment.

Bride: I still want a long-standing committed relationship. I just don't happen to think that commitment is synonymous with marriage.

Mom: So, you want a long-standing committed *but not-married* relationship?

Bride: Yeah.

Mom: With Mark.

Bride: Right.

[The minister enters, wearing an alb and stole.]

Minister: Is everything all right here?

Mom: Oh, thank goodness you're here. My daughter is trying to call off the wedding. Tell her why marriage is a good thing.

Minister: Oh, um, well… Whenever people come together in love, that's part of God's plan. According to tradition, marriage is a sacred union, ordained by God and blessed by the church. The covenant of marriage is symbolically parallel to the covenant between God and God's people. And finally, some would argue, if it weren't for marriage, people would be having sex left, right, and center, and we'd never get any work done… Anything there change your mind?

Bride: Not really.

Minister: OK then. I hate acting as an intermediary for the state anyway.

[The minister takes off the alb and stole.]

Minister: You should still have a party, though. Parties are good.

[The minister leaves.]

Mom: That was not helpful… So, what are you going to call him?

Bride: Who?

Mom: Mark. The man you don't want to marry. You're at a party, introducing him to some friends, and you say, "This is my…"

Bride: …"Mark"?

Mom: You can't say, "This is my Mark." It sounds like a line from *Guys and Dolls*.

Bride: If I had to call him something, I'd call him my partner.

> [As she speaks, Mom starts taking the bride's jacket off and easing her back into the dress.]

Mom: I'm not trying to scare you, but I've seen this happen before. You start off with wonderful intentions. "This is my partner. Have you met my partner? My partner, Mark." But then you run into people who ask what business you're in. So you'll try "life partner," but it will feel awkward and wordy. Or like a code-word you have no right using. And then you'll start slipping into "spouse." A little bit clearer, a little more familiar. But people will hear "spouse" and *think* "husband." And then, eventually, you'll be talking to people who don't know you, and you won't feel like explaining the whole story, so you'll just call him "husband." Just for simplicity's sake. And then one day, you'll realize, he *is* your husband. And you're his wife. And there's nothing radical about your relationship after all. You're just the same as the married couple that lives next door. Except you never got to wear the dress. And you never had the special day. And you'll regret it.

> [The bride is now back in the wedding gown and standing in front of the mirror.]

Mom: There, now. What do you see?

Bride: Me.

Mom: What kind of you?

> [The bride is becoming entranced by her own image.]

Bride: A beautiful me.

Mom: The most beautiful you in the world. You're gorgeous.

Bride: Like a princess.

Mom: Every woman deserves to be seen as a princess, at least once; to have everyone recognize the grace, the nobility… And think about once you're married, walking down the street with Mark, arm in arm. Every once in a while you hold hands and your rings clink together. People look at you and say, "What a lovely young couple." Lonely people are envious of your happiness. Everyone wants to be like you. You're young, and you're together, and you represent everything that is good and hopeful in the world… And then when you have children, they'll say, "What a beautiful family. You must be so proud." …And when you are old, with your husband of 50 years, and all your children and grandchildren around you, you will look at your family and think, "What an accomplishment! What a wonderful thing I have made." …That's what happiness is, my darling. That's what this day is about.

[The bride stares at the mirror, captivated by the vision her mother has created. Suddenly, with a jump back, she snaps out of it.]

Bride: Holy geez, that's addictive! Wow! The childhood dream of living up to everyone's expectations. It's *scary* how good that feels. It's like crack cocaine, it just… Whoa!

[She quickly climbs out of the dress.]

Bride: I mean, talk about your enhanced sense of self-esteem. I could *feel* the analytical skills draining out of me.

Mom: All right, young lady, a lot of people have put money and effort into making this event happen, so you're going to put that dress back on and you're going to march yourself down that aisle and get married!

[Slight pause.]

Bride: You know, Mom, that didn't work when I was a kid.

[The bride continues getting out of the wedding gown.]

Mom: Why are you doing this to me?!

Bride: Why is this so important to you?

[Mom sits on the chair.]

Mom: You were young when your father and I divorced. You maybe don't remember much about it.

[The bride kneels beside her mom.]

Mom: Everyone at church was very kind, very supportive. They took good care of us. But when it came time to find greeters for Sunday morning, they thought of the Lewis family, the Mitchell family, the Carney family. And then they thought of "Maureen and her kids." And again for lighting the Advent candles – the Munroe family, the Wilson family, "Maureen and her children." We weren't a family anymore, we were a woman and her kids. It wasn't meant as a putdown. It wasn't meant as *anything*; it was just a way of speaking. It certainly wasn't intended to hurt… But it's a shock when you realize that you're not a real family anymore.

[The bride takes her hand.]

Mom: I tried to shield you kids from it. I didn't want you to think of yourselves as any different, even if everyone else looked at us differently. I wanted you to grow up happy… You see, Janie, that's why this is important. You have a chance to start a real family. You have a chance to be happy.

Bride: But, Mom, we *had* a *real* family. There was never anything for you to be ashamed of. Nobody has a mom, a dad, two-point-five kids, and a dog. But we furiously hold on to this narrow definition of the traditional family, and we feel guilty when we don't live up to it. *That's* why I can't get married, Mom. Getting married would be buying into a belief system where the only *real* family is one that is started by a husband and a wife. So my gay and lesbian friends aren't really family. And divorced people aren't family. And people who choose not to have children aren't family. And people who live together and support each other in any other ways, aren't family. It's an exclusive club, and I don't want membership unless everyone else gets it as well.

Mom: Honey, you know that I admire your convictions and I think it's great that you're worried about your friends, and that you want to stand up for gays and lesbians and divorced people and couples without children and the whole works... But you don't have to be like those people. You're *normal*.

[The bride gets up and puts the jeans and jacket on.]

Bride: I could have this gorgeous ceremony. Everyone would be overjoyed for me. I could have a "real" husband and a "real" family and all the things that people consider normal. I could see my life reflected on TV. I could have my interests upheld in the legislature. I could have my values affirmed in the media and the church. Why do I deserve that? Because, by some fluke of biology and random chance I happen to be heterosexual and Mark happens to be heterosexual and we happened to find each other and happened to want to spend our lives together? For this I should be rewarded? Not for anything I've done, but for what I am? Or, more precisely, for what I'm *not*? If this is what it means to be a "normal" family, Mom, I don't want it... Mark and I are going to have a party now, to celebrate not being married.

[She leaves.]

Mom: Janie...? Jane...?

[She looks wistfully at the dress, lying in a pile on the ground. Pause. She starts to put the dress on.]

Mom: Well, *somebody's* going to get married today!

[The end.]

LEGEND OF SAINT ANDREW

A Miracle Play

PROLOGUE

[The Actor enters. He acts as narrator and sets the scene.]

Actor: When winter winds blow icy cold

and all seek comfort from their chills,

then is the time to act out tales

of holy saints and miracles.

When summer blooms, and festivals

call common folk to sing and dance,

then is the time to see saint plays

for guidance and for sustenance.

So come, good people, gather round,

an ancient legend, told anew,

of holy folk and holy acts

and one whose name is known to you –

Saint Andrew!

[Saint Andrew enters, a large, intensely serious man.]

Actor: This is Saint Andrew, here portrayed,

a saintly man, both kind and good,

a man of virtue, perfect, pure,

who does all things a Christian should.

SCENE 1: MATTHIAS INDUCTED INTO THE APOSTLES' CLUB

[Saint Andrew sits in the corner and reads a newspaper.]

Actor: Our story starts after the death

and resurrection of Our Lord,

whose life was crushed upon the cross.

But then, by God, Life was restored.

Now Pentecost has come and gone,

and now an Early Church is born.

Saint Andrew and his cohort saints

are gathered in one place this morn.

[The Actor steps aside to reveal the Apostles' Club. The various apostles and saints enter and sit around, drinking brandy, playing cards, conversing, reading. Saint Peter enters, leading Saint Matthias.]

Peter: And this is the Apostles' Club. Gentlemen, this is Saint Matthias, our latest apostle. He'll be replacing Judas Iscariot.

[At the sound of Judas' name, all the apostles mutter "Judas" and spit on the floor. Bartholomew extends his hand to Matthias.]

Bartholomew: Welcome to the club, old chap. I'm sure you'll be a topnotch apostle.

Matthias: [nervously] I certainly hope so.

[Saint Peter pats Matthias on the shoulder.]

Peter: You'll fit in just fine, Matthias. After all, we wouldn't have chosen you if we didn't think you had the "right stuff," apostolically speaking.

[Saint Peter leaves Matthias with Bartholomew and Thomas.]

Thomas: We're having a euchre round-robin this afternoon. Matthew, Mark, and Luke need a fourth.

Bartholomew: They used to play with Saint John, but he kept going alone. Terribly annoying.

Thomas: Are you in?

Matthias: Well, sure. That sounds great.

Thomas: Smashing!

Bartholomew: Now, who haven't you met? Saint James?

Thomas: Dull. Simon the Zealot?

Bartholomew: Don't mention the Romans, you'll be there for hours.

Matthias: Who's that in the corner?

[All look to Saint Andrew, sitting in the corner, alone, reading a newspaper.]

Bartholomew: Ah, the old man himself, Saint Andrew.

Matthias: Oh my gosh! I've heard so much about him, I never thought I'd ever get to meet him. I mean, he's the first apostle. He's like... Wow!

[Thomas and Bartholomew give each other a look.]

Thomas: Yes, he certainly is that.

Matthias: Do you suppose I could go and say hello to him?

Bartholomew: You're a member of the Apostles' Club now, my boy. You can do anything you please.

[Matthias nervously approaches Saint Andrew. Saint Andrew continues reading his paper. Matthias stands for a moment, gathering his nerve, and then speaks.]

Matthias: Um, hello. Andrew? Mister Andrew. Saint Andrew...sir. I just wanted to say that it's a great honor to finally meet you after all these years of... Well, it's a very great honor, and I've always sort of looked up to you, and hoped that some day I could be an apostle, just like you. And, well, here I am! ...Which is not to say that I'm in any way of the same order of magnitude as you are. I just meant to say that, well, I'm very proud to be an apostle. No, not proud. *Pleased.* Actually, anxious. I'm quite nervous about the whole thing, because, well, here are all these wonderful saints, and can I live up to the kind of expectations that go with being a saint? I mean, it's an awful lot of pressure, don't you think?

[Saint Andrew, for the first time, turns from his paper. He stares impassively at Matthias for a moment, then turns back to his paper without speaking a word. Pause. Matthias opens his mouth to speak, but instead he slinks back to Bartholomew and Thomas.]

Bartholomew: Andy can be a bit of a grump.

Matthias: Does he ever talk?

Thomas: Yes, but to be quite honest we prefer his silence.

Matthias: Is he like that with everybody?

Bartholomew: Ironically, he got on fairly well with Judas Iscariot.

[All the apostles mutter "Judas" and spit. Saint Peter moves to the middle of the room to make an announcement.]

Peter: Gentlemen, gentlemen, if I could have your attention. I have an announcement. This shouldn't take more than – whoa…!

[Peter slips on the spit-covered floor, but catches his balance.]

Peter: All right, *two* announcements. First, enough spitting. It's quite clear how we feel about Judas, and furthermore the custodian is starting to complain. Second announcement: I believe we've been basking in our pentecostal splendor long enough. If you'll recall, our good rabbi once sent us out into the world, and I think it's time for us to do that once again; to go forth to the four corners of the world, performing miracles and proclaiming Jesus, our poor murdered teacher and our glorious messiah.

[Saint Andrew throws down his paper and jumps up.]

Andrew: About time!

Thomas: Euchre game's off.

Peter: Now, I have established a system…

Bartholomew: [aside to Thomas] Who died and made him pope?

Peter: …whereby each of us goes out with a partner. Barnabas will go to Tarsus to join Paul. James and John can go together…

Thomas: [whining] James and John always get to go together!

Peter: Bartholomew and Thomas.

Bartholomew and Thomas: [like kids] Yay!

Peter: Saint Andrew, our first apostle, will go with…

[All the apostles avoid eye-contact with Peter, hoping not to get picked.]

Peter: Matthias, our latest apostle.

[Matthias looks to Bartholomew and Thomas. They shrug sympathetically. Saint Andrew grabs Matthias' hand and strides off.]

Andrew: Come.

Peter: On your way, O saints of God, and may Christ be with you to the ends of the earth.

[The apostles leave as the Actor enters, carrying a small wooden boat.]

SCENE 2: ANDREW CONFRONTS THE KING OF BYZANTIUM

> **Actor:** Jerusalem is bid farewell,
>
> as our two saints set off in search
>
> of sinners seeking God's Good News
>
> and converts for the newborn church.
>
> [The illusion of water is created by two people holding the ends of a blue strip of cloth. Over this "sea" the Actor sails a small toy boat.]

> **Actor:** Two holy men upon the sea,
>
> a fishing boat upon the wave,
>
> pilgrims to a waiting world,
>
> fishermen of souls to save.
>
> [Saint Andrew and Matthias on a small sailing boat. They stand in front of the "sea" cloth. A mast and sail could be erected to create the illusion. Andrew is at the rudder, looking straight out at the horizon, his gaze unwavering.]

> **Matthias:** So, I guess you learned to pilot a boat when you were a fisherman, right? I think I remember reading somewhere that you were a fisher. You and your brother Peter. You know, you and Peter don't look much alike at all. Do you get that a lot...? Does anyone ever call you "Drew"...? I think it's great that we're going out in pairs. That collegial spirit is really what I was looking forward to as an apostle. That sense of teamwork, mutual support.
>
> [Andrew stares straight ahead, not acknowledging Matthias. Pause.]

> **Matthias:** ...You realize, do you, that we've been in this boat for nearly a week and you haven't said a single word? Except for that one time the sail was swinging around, and you said, "duck" – which I really do appreciate. It's just that I was hoping that we could use the travel time to get to know each other. Enter into some kind of a dialogue. A conversation. A kind of thing where I say something and then...*you* say something. Do you see what I'm getting at here?
>
> [Pause.]

> **Matthias:** Andrew. Saint Andrew?
>
> [Andrew looks at him.]

> **Matthias:** I just need to ask – have I done something to offend you?
>
> [Andrew shakes his head.]

Matthias: So it's just that we haven't developed a level of trust that would allow you to open up?

[Andrew shakes his head.]

Matthias: So, it's just that you have no interest whatsoever in talking to me?

[Andrew nods.]

Matthias: OK… This is going to be a long trip.

[Zeuxippos, king of Byzantium, enters and stands a distance away from Andrew and Matthias, holding a spear.]

Actor: Upon this city's wall, a man,

Zeuxippos his regal name.

He stands in kingly majesty,

Byzantium is his domain.

Zeux: [calling to Matthias and Andrew] I got my spear trained right on the bridge of yer nose, so y'all just keep on sailin'. We don't need none of yer kind around here.

Matthias: I am Saint Matthias and this is Saint Andrew. We are apostles of Jesus the Christ.

Zeux: I knows who y'are and I knows *what* y'are. And like I said, folks around these parts don't wants to be bothered by the likes of yous.

Matthias: Let me assure you, sir, we have only goodwill…

Zeux: Are you talkin' back to me, son?

Matthias: No, sir. I'm just trying to allay your fears that…

Zeux: Do you know who you're talkin' to?

Matthias: No, sir, we haven't been properly…

Zeux: My name's Zeuxippos. Z-E-U-X-I-P-P-O-S, Zeuxippos. And this here's my city. I am king of Byzantium. Do ye hear what I'm sayin'? Do ye git what I'm meanin'? I am king, which means what I says goes. So if I says you and yer friend gonna keep on movin', keep on movin' is what you and yer friend is gonna do.

Matthias: Obviously we'll respect your wishes, but we mean you no harm. We are only good Christian saints, out in the world to spread the good news of…

Zeux: No harm!? We bin plagued by you evangelical types for weeks! Always showin' up at the city gate on a Saturday mornin', 'fore anybody's up and had their cup of coffee yet. Always smilin' and askin' if'n we wants to read any of yer literature. It's Saturday mornin', fer God's sake! It's the only day we gets to sleep in!

Matthias: We understand. Sorry to have bothered you. [to Andrew] Maybe we should change course slightly and head up into the Black Sea.

[Andrew does not move to change course.]

Matthias: …Andrew?

[Andrew keeps looking straight ahead, not changing course.]

Zeux: I see y'all are still gettin' closer to Byzantium. Maybe I didn't make myself clear.

Matthias: Well, thank you anyway for your time. We'll be on our way now. [turning back to Andrew] Saint Andrew?

[Andrew is still heading straight for Byzantium.]

Zeux: We've had 40 of you Christians come knockin' on our gates, and if y'all look over the edge of yer boat, ye'll see all 40 of 'em at the bottom of the sea. Y'all wantin' to make that 42?

Matthias: Saint Andrew, I really think we ought to leave.

[Andrew does not budge. Matthias tries wrestling the rudder away from Andrew, to no avail.]

Zeux: I'm warning you.

Matthias: Don't worry, everything's under control.

Zeux: I'm not talking to hear the sound of my own voice here, boys. You come within ten feet of the city and I'll have ye drowned like the rest of them holy door-knockers at the bottom of the sea.

[Saint Andrew beaches the boat. He gets out and stands before the city.]

Andrew: Zeuxippos, obstructive king of Byzantium, hear me. I am Saint Andrew, follower of the Christ. I will not approach your gates. I will not enter your city. But today, with the stones of this beach, I am making a church.

[Andrew starts to build a church of stones.]

Andrew: You are under siege, Zeuxippos. Soon your people will starve for want of spiritual food, and the good news of Jesus Christ will break through your city walls. Then your kingdom will be lost to you forever.

Zeux: That area's not properly zoned fer churches. I'll have you thrown into the sea and drowned.

Matthias: Saint Andrew, what are you doing? We can't build a church when there's no congregation?

Andrew: Zeuxippos has made our congregation for us. A congregation of 40.

[Andrew waves his hands over the water and prays.]

Andrew: God, raise your dead servants from the bottom of the sea. Complete the baptism of your Byzantine congregation.

[The Actor makes a mysterious sound on a musical instrument (wind chimes, flute, harp?). People come rising out of the sea, walking out from behind the strip of blue cloth. (This can also be done by drawing little faces on the fingers of the people holding the blue cloth and having the "finger people" rise from the sea.)]

Andrew: This is the congregation of First Church Byzantium, Zeuxippos. Their mission is to plague you day and night. You will realize that your petty authority is nothing compared with the awesome power of God.

[Andrew gets back in the boat.]

Andrew: Come Matthias, we're going.

[The Actor sails the boat over the sea again. The recently resurrected evangelists gather around Zeuxippos.]

Matthias: You're not one of those saints with a death-wish, are you?

Zeux: [calling after them] You can't do this, Saint Andrew! I'm the king around here! I'm in charge! …All right all you resurrected people, back in the sea where you belong!

Actor: Having built a church and raised up those

who by the tyrant had been drowned,

Saint Andrew and Matthias leave,

and make their way to foreign ground.

[Zeuxippos, the drowned people, the Actor, and the "sea" leave.]

SCENE 3: ANDREW AND MATTHIAS IN THE LAND OF BARBARIANS

[Matthias and Saint Andrew are on foot now.]

Matthias: Just for future reference, you can catch more flies with honey…

Andrew: We don't want flies.

Matthias: No, of course we don't want flies…

Andrew: Then why are you talking about flies?

Matthias: I'm talking about trying not to alienate people. Your confrontational style… Hey, wait a minute. Are we in Scythia?

[Andrew nods.]

Matthias: Don't you know that Scythia is where the barbarians live?! It's cold and desolate and hostile territory.

[Andrew nods.]

Matthias: Listen, you have to be more diplomatic if we're going to be dealing with barbarians. It doesn't take much to set them off. Can you promise me that you'll at least *try* not to get us killed?

[Andrew shakes his head.]

Matthias: Look, there's a town up ahead. Let me show you what I mean.

[Saint Andrew and Matthias approach a town. The mayor enters and calls out to them.]

Mayor: Halt, travelers! Don't come any further.

Matthias: I assure you, gentle townsperson, that we mean you no harm. We are apostles of Jesus, the savior. We come bringing good news and saving acts.

Mayor: That's all well and good, but unless you can cast out demons it's not safe for you to come through these gates.

Matthias: As a matter of fact, we *can* cast out demons. [to Andrew] Can't we?

[Andrew nods.]

Mayor: Then, noble saints, you are welcome here.

Matthias: [to Andrew] See? If you're friendly and polite, and you give the people what they want, everything works out smoothly.

[They enter the town. Townspeople enter to watch the action.]

Mayor: The demon takes the form of a devil-dog and attacks everyone who comes through the town gates. It's really been putting a crimp in our tourism industry. Look!

[The townspeople gasp as the demon-dog enters. The "demon" is a cute puppy dog, played by an actor with a dog puppet.]

Matthias: Aww.

Mayor: Don't go "aww." It's a vicious devil, who has killed seven of our townspeople already.

Matthias: Of course, I'm sorry. [taking Andrew aside] Obviously, there's some underlying socio-economic tension plaguing this community, which these people are projecting onto this innocent puppy dog. The real demon is fear and unresolved anxiety. [to the townspeople] Good people, watch. This dog does not need to be your enemy. Only let it know that it can trust you, and it will be your friend for life.

[Matthias approaches the dog, holding his hand out.]

Matthias: Good puppy. Good puppy. You're a nice dog, aren't you. Don't worry, I'm not going to hurt you. Here, sniff my hand. That's a good boy. There, see?

[The dog sniffs Matthias' hand, then pants playfully. Matthias scratches it on the head.]

Matthias: You're a good puppy, aren't you. Yes, you are. Yes, you are! [to townspeople] See? No demon here. Just a dog who wants to be loved.

[The dog lets out a deep rumbling growl and chomps down hard on Matthias' arm. Matthias tries to pull and shake it off, but the devil-dog will not let go.]

Matthias: Yeeow!

Mayor: I told you it was a demon.

Matthias: Ow, ow, ow, ow! Youch, that hurts!

Mayor: I mean, look at that tail.

[The mayor holds up the devil's pointy red tail. The demon releases Matthias' arm briefly to threaten the mayor.]

Demon: [in a deep, growly voice] Don't touch the tail.

[The demon-dog chomps back down on Matthias's arm.]

Matthias: Agh! Wow, that really… Yow!! Son of a bitch!

Andrew: Do you want me to cast it out for you?

Matthias: No, no. Ow! I can do it, I'm an apostle. Owee, owee, owee, owee! [to demon] Um, demon, I would like to…could you just, would you just… OK, demon, I would like to invite you to consider entering into a time of letting go of my arm. All right?

Demon: Grr!

Andrew: Do you want me to do it?

Matthias: No, thank you! I can handle it! Now, devil, I'm hearing anger in your voice. Is that an accurate reading?

Demon: Grrr!

Matthias: OW, OW, OW! OK, good. Now, I want you to consider letting go of the things that are holding you back in your spiritual growth – your anger, the need to attack townspeople…my arm! If that feels like something you want to do.

Demon: Grr!

Matthias: Yow! Ow! Yikes! Holy smokes, that hurts!

Andrew: Do you want me to…

Matthias: Yes! Do it!

> [Andrew slams his fist down on top of the devil-dog's head. The demon yelps and lets go of Matthias' arm.]

Demon: [menacingly] Saint Andrew.

Andrew: Demon! By the power of God I cast thee out. Leave this town, NOW!!

> [The demon growls and stares at Saint Andrew for a moment.]

Andrew: [threatening] By the power of God…!

> [The demon relents, and leaves quickly.]

Townsperson: Saint Andrew, you've saved our town.

Andrew: You don't negotiate with devils.

Matthias: [conceding] Right.

Andrew: You look them in the eye and you tell them what to do.

> [A traveler from down the road enters.]

Traveler: Hey, you'll never guess what happened. I was just at the next town down the road and this devil-dog swooped down from the sky and just killed this guy. It was the weirdest thing, because that town's never had a problem with demons before. This devil-dog just came out of nowhere.

[Andrew and Matthias look at each other.]

Andrew: We'll go there next.

Matthias: Right.

Mayor: You are indeed holy men. You will win many souls in this town with your miraculous powers. [indicating a pregnant townsperson] This woman has been pregnant these past two years, but she is unable to give birth. It is very painful. Could you comfort her?

[Matthias goes to the pregnant woman. (A soft doll or puppet, rolled up and hidden under her skirt should create the illusion.) Matthias sits down beside her, and holds her hand. He sits there for a long time, smiling at the woman and nodding.]

Andrew: What are you doing?

Matthias: Ministry of presence. I'm being with her in her pain... [to woman] Do you feel ministered to?

Woman: Contraction!!

[The woman feels a labor pain and grabs Matthias' arm.]

Matthias: Ah, oh! Not the arm again!

Andrew: [getting ready to knock the woman on the head] Do you want some help?

Matthias: No!! No, I can handle it.

[Matthias extracts his arm from the woman's grip.]

Matthias: Now, good woman, tell me how you feel.

Woman: Oh holy saint, I have been in constant labor pain for more than a year. Tell me, what have I done to be punished in this way?

Matthias: Oh, dear woman, God is not punishing you. God is with you, suffering every pain that grips you.

Woman: But can't you make it stop? I'll do whatever you ask, just get this baby out of me. [grabbing Matthias by the collar] I'm serious. I want this baby out NOW!

Matthias: I understand, ma'am. My friend, Saint Andrew, is blessed with the power to heal, and if you just, let, go, of my shirt I'm sure he'd be happy to help you. Wouldn't you, Saint Andrew.

Andrew: No.

Matthias: Andrew?

Andrew: No.

Matthias: What he means is that he *himself* can't heal you, but God can heal you through him. Andrew's very modest. Isn't that right, Andrew.

Andrew: No.

Mayor: What kind of saints are you, won't heal a woman who needs your help?

Andrew: [to the woman] What does your husband do?

Matthias: What does her husband have to do with it?

Andrew: Your husband is an assassin, isn't he. He kills for money.

Woman: [ashamed] Yes.

Andrew: You will not give birth to this child unless you reject your evils ways, repent your sins, and turn to God.

Woman: Must I be punished for my husband's sins? Is this how your God operates?

Matthias: No. No, it's not. Saint Andrew, could I have a word with you a moment?

Andrew: You are married to your husband, and therefore married to his sin. You have built your lifestyle on his blood money. His murders pay for your luxuries. Unless you extract yourself from this ill-gotten comfort and seek God's mercy, unless you leave your husband and devote your life to Jesus the Christ, your labor pains will never cease.

Matthias: Andrew?

Andrew: Your unborn child wants life, but you have chosen to make a happy home for death! As long as you remain complicit to greedy murder, your child will stay lodged in your gut!

Matthias: Andrew!

> [Matthias drags Andrew aside. The woman stays behind, crying. Halfway through the conversation, she begins to pray silently.]

Matthias: What do you think you're doing?!? I'm trying to comfort this woman, and you're telling her that her sinfulness is the cause of her excruciating pain. You're totally contradicting everything I'm trying to do, and you're, you're… you're blaming the victim! Which is… I mean, my God, where did you study pastoral care?!? You just told the woman to leave her husband, without knowing anything about her! That was the most heavy-handed, bullying abuse of power I've ever seen. I just, I just, I just, I can't believe it!

[Slight pause.]

Andrew: Are you done?

Matthias: For now, I think, yes.

Andrew: Good.

[The woman yells as she has a labor pain.]

Woman: Whoa!

Matthias: What?

Woman: It's coming. It's time.

[Matthias and Andrew rush to her.]

Matthias: OK, breathe, breathe.

Woman: I did what you said. I prayed to God and asked forgiveness, and I decided to give my life to Jesus, and suddenly - WHOA!

[The woman gives birth. Andrew pulls the "baby" from her skirt and hands it to her.]

Andrew: You are the mother of a beautiful and healthy 37-pound boy.

Woman: Bless you, sir. Tell me your name.

Andrew: I am Saint Andrew.

Woman: [to the baby] My son, in honor of the holy man who made your birth possible, I will name you after him. You will be named "Saint."

Matthias: [fuming] I need a drink.

[Matthias moves off to the side. The Actor pours a glass of water and hands it to him. A crowd gathers around Saint Andrew.]

Matthias: [to himself] This isn't working out at all like I expected. I applied for the apostle position because I wanted to go out and make friends with the world; I wanted to preach the gospel of love and compassion; I wanted to tell people about kind and gentle Jesus. But instead I get stuck with this confrontational, insensitive shock-trooper of a saint, who seems bent on getting us in trouble and alienating everyone we meet. I mean, come on. Telling a woman that leaving her husband and rejecting evil will cure her?! ...And that it worked?! I mean, sure, I was expecting some differences in working style, even theological differences. But this is too much! I think this whole partner thing was a mistake. Maybe we should just wish each other well and go our separate ways, and...

[During Matthias's soliloquy an argument breaks out between Andrew and the townspeople. Matthias rushes over, still carrying the glass of water. All the townspeople are yelling at Saint Andrew.]

Townsperson 1: Who do you think you are? What gives you the right?

Andrew: God gives me the right!

Matthias: What's going on?

Townsperson 2: We oughta string him up. That's what we did in the old days.

Townsperson 3: Home-wrecker! We used to be happy before you came to town!

Andrew: Idolatrous fools! When our Lord Jesus returns to judge...

Townsperson 1: Shut up! You've caused enough trouble!

Matthias: Hey. Hey! What's going on?

Townsperson 1: This so-called saint broke up my daughter's wedding. He said the bride and groom were too closely related, then he sent my daughter off to a convent. Do you know how much we spent on that wedding?

Townsperson 3: He stole my son!

Andrew: Your child has chosen to be a follower of the Christ!

Townsperson 3: And now our boy won't come home with his own mother and father.

Townsperson 1: We believe in family values around here, mister.

Andrew: The only values are the values of God! All others are of the Devil and will burn away in the coming fire!

Townsperson 2: I'll show *you* a coming fire!

Townsperson 3: You have no respect for the sanctity of the family!

Andrew: When was the family ever sanctified? You are worshippers of idols and the penalty for idolatry is death! Repent your evil ways!

Townsperson 2: [making it up on the spot] He turned my sister-in-law into a chicken!

Townsperson 3: Really?

Townsperson 2: …Yeah.

Townsperson 1: Sorcerer!!

Townsperson 3: Burn him!

Townsperson 2: [pointing at Matthias] Hey, that guy's his friend. Grab him, too; we'll burn them both.

[Matthias takes quick action, trying to placate the townspeople.]

Matthias: Wait! [grabbing a boy and giving him to Townsperson 3] Look, here's your son, take him. [to Townsperson 1] And you, tell your family that the wedding's back on. We're sorry for any inconvenience, and we hope the grandkids turn out OK. All of you, I apologize for anything my friend may have said or done. We don't want any trouble, we'll just be on our way.

[Slight pause.]

Townsperson 2: Burn them anyway!

[Two of the townspeople grab Andrew and Matthias. Townsperson 1 gets a torch (perhaps a piece of red cloth on a stick) and starts approaching Andrew and Matthias. Andrew grabs the glass of water out of Matthias' hand and throws it on the torch, extinguishing it.]

Townsperson 3: He put the torch out!

Townsperson 2: They *are* sorcerers!

Townsperson 1: Their Jesus is too powerful for us. Run away! Run away!

[The crowd of townspeople runs away. Pause.]

Andrew: Come.

[Andrew starts to stride towards the next town. Matthias doesn't move. Andrew looks back at Matthias. Matthias shakes his head, and leaves. Alone. Saint Andrew watches him go. The Actor enters.]

Actor: So Matthias and Saint Andrew split

to separate corners of the earth,

yet neither ceased to tell the tale

of Christ's life, death, and rebirth.

SCENE 4: MATTHIAS CAPTURED BY CANNIBALS

Actor: To the City of Dogs, Sevastopol,

far to the North, our tale proceeds.

On his own Matthias comes

with gentle words and kindly deeds.

Alas, the cannibals of this domain

care little for his gospel zeal.

They will not hear Matthias speak.

They'd rather have him for their meal.

And so our well-intentioned saint

is roughly captured, bound, and beaten,

and thrown into a dungeon dark,

to sit and wait 'til he is eaten.

[Matthias enters, with a blood-soaked bandage wrapped around his eyes. He paces around a small cell. An angel appears.]

Angel: Fear not, gentle Matthias.

Matthias: Who's there? I can't see.

Angel: I am an angel sent by God.

Matthias: God be praised!

Angel: I will help you to escape.

Matthias: Bless you, angel.

Angel: I have summoned Saint Andrew to come and rescue you.

Matthias: Never mind then. Thanks anyway.

Angel: But you have been captured by cannibals, and they mean to eat you.

Matthias: Yeah, I know, but I'm coming to terms with it.

[Andrew rushes in and stops outside the "door" to Matthias' cell.]

Andrew: Matthias, I have come to save you.

Matthias: No thanks.

Andrew: Stand back as I break down the door.

> [Andrew throws his whole weight against the cell door. The door does not budge.]

Matthias: Thanks anyway, Andrew. I've got everything under control.

> [Andrew rushes at the door again. No effect.]

Andrew: God in heaven, by your holy power, make this door open to me!

Angel: Andrew.

> [Andrew bashes the door again, and again, other than hurting his shoulder, it has no effect.]

Angel: Andrew.

Andrew: Yes, blessed angel.

Angel: It's not locked.

Andrew: Oh.

> [Andrew turns the handle and enters. He gasps at the sight of Matthias, beaten and blinded.]

Andrew: Oh, Matthias! How did you get here?

Matthias: Get where?

Andrew: In this cell. Beaten and blinded by vicious cannibals.

Matthias: Oh that. I don't know. The last thing I remember was discussing the theology of incarnation with the king of Murgundia. Then he offered me a frothy drink, which was quite tasty as I recall. Then he started showing me flow charts and graphs...

Andrew: Graphs.

Matthias: Yes. You see, they've got quite an ingenious system here. They keep track of the projected earnings and productivity for each person living in the kingdom, and those who don't compete to a certain standard get eaten. Makes sense, really, if you think about it. Anyway, I guess I must have drifted off, because the next thing I remember, I was here. In the dark.

Andrew: Come. We'll escape before the cannibals return.

Matthias: No thanks. Cannibalism is a well-established part of Murgundian culture and it would be insensitive not to be eaten. Not that I'd expect *you* to understand sensitivity.

Angel: I fear the cannibals have drugged him to make him complacent.

[Andrew puts his hands on Matthias' head and prays.]

Andrew: God, restore the sight and clear the mind of your servant, Matthias.

[Actor plays the "miracle instrument." Andrew pulls the cloth off Matthias' eyes. Matthias blinks and looks around.]

Matthias: On the other hand, leaving might not be an inappropriate course of action.

[Andrew and Matthias start to leave. A cannibal with a spear enters.]

Cannibal: Hey, where are you going with our lunch?

[The angel blocks the cannibal's way.]

Angel: Hurry and escape. I'll hold the cannibal at bay with my flaming sword.

Cannibal: What flaming sword?

Angel: Oh, did I forget the flaming sword? Fine, I'll just buffet you around the head with my wings, so stay back.

Andrew: [pulling Matthias] Come.

Cannibal: This isn't fair. We've already posted the menu.

Matthias: Not fair?! Not fair! You were going to eat me!

Cannibal: Sure, but it's not like we kept you in a fattening pen your whole life.

Matthias: It's sick and it's immoral!

Cannibal: Oh, if that's not cultural imperialism I don't know what is.

[Matthias starts to walk back to the cannibal.]

Matthias: I guess you've got a point there.

Andrew: Matthias!

[Matthias snaps out of it, turns and moves back toward Saint Andrew.]

Matthias: Right! [to cannibal] People aren't livestock, you big jerk!

Cannibal: You're really letting us down here, Matthias.

[Matthias stops and turns back toward the cannibal.]

Andrew: Matthias!

[Andrew picks up Matthias and starts to carry him off. The cannibal looks at the angel.]

Cannibal: Hmm. Angel food cake.

[The angel runs away, pursued by the cannibal. The Actor enters with the small boat.]

Actor: Fleeing hungry cannibals

and their all-consuming lust for blood,

the comrade saints set sail once more,

determined not to be their food.

[Andrew and Matthias "sail" in. Andrew, as usual, is staring straight ahead, steering the boat.]

Matthias: You traveled halfway across the world just because you heard I was in danger. Maybe it's just the cannibal drugs in my system, but…I'm touched. I can't help but think that maybe this is a turning point in our relationship, that this shared threat has created a bond between us, and that now, maybe, we can open up and express our feelings.

[Pause. Andrew continues to drive the boat forward, not responding to Matthias.]

Matthias: [sighing] On the other hand…

[Andrew glances at Matthias, then looks back at the horizon. Pause.]

Andrew: …I was a disciple of the Baptist. And then they killed him.

[Pause. Finally…]

Andrew: I was a disciple of the Christ. They killed him too.

[Pause.]

Andrew: I was a coward when I went into the wilderness. John taught me to be a "son of thunder." I told him I was afraid of death. He told me I was afraid of life, and he pushed me under the water until my lungs were ready to explode. He showed me the fine line between life and death. Then the Rabbi came and I was the first to follow.

[Pause.]

Andrew: They killed the Baptist. And then they killed the Rabbi.

[Andrew continues to look straight ahead. Matthias looks at him. Pause.]

Matthias: Just because you haven't been killed doesn't mean you're a failure.

[Andrew does not respond.]

Matthias: Andrew?

SCENE 5: THE MARTYRDOM OF SAINT ANDREW

Actor: Bold Andrew is a driven man,

seeking neither rest nor peace.

From Scythia to Epirus,

and then from Epirus to Greece.

After Greece they hit Nicea,

then Gorsinia and Galatia,

Tauria, Bithnia, Iberia, Sogdinia,

Cappadocia, and Sauromatia.

In all these places Andrew preaches,

undiluted, unashamed.

Until they come to that locale

in southern Greece, Achaia named.

[Andrew and Matthias arrive at the city. Aegeus, the proconsul, enters, in a well-tailored business suit. He smiles like a smarmy politician.]

Aegeus: Saint Andrew, how you doing? Aegeus, proconsul of Achaia. I hear it through the grapevine that you've been preaching some noxious heresy with underlying political implications.

Andrew: I preach the good news of Jesus Christ.

Aegeus: Hey, nothing wrong with that, as long as it doesn't get out of hand, right? I'll tell you what…

[He leads Andrew to a place where some idols are set up.]

Aegeus: You see these idols here? Make a little sacrifice to them, and we're square. Sound good?

[Andrew glares at Aegeus.]

Aegeus: Saint – may I call you Saint? – Saint, these idols represent stability, security, fiscal responsibility, positive reviews by the international banking community. We've been worshipping these idols for as long as anyone in my government can remember… which is about four or five years. There's nothing sacrilegious about sacrificing to them.

Andrew: I will not worship graven images.

Aegeus: Please don't challenge my authority, Saint.

Andrew: The only authority is God.

[Pause.]

Aegeus: Fine. The only thing the public hates more than a brutal tyrant is a wimp, so…

[A soldier enters with a length of rope.]

Aegeus: [to soldier] Prepare the saint for crucifixion.

[The soldier wraps the rope around Andrew's wrists and starts to lead him off.]

Matthias: Don't worry, Andrew. We have supporters in this city. I'll rally them, and we'll get a whole army to rise up and rescue you.

Andrew: No. If this is God's will…

Matthias: But…

Andrew: No!

Matthias: But you got to rescue me.

[Andrew puts his hands on Matthias' shoulder.]

Andrew: You're a good saint, Matthias.

[The soldier leads Andrew off. Matthias watches him go, then leaves in the opposite direction. The Actor enters, holding a rough wooden X-shaped cross.]

Actor: Like some roguish criminal

our noble saint is guilty found,

and to an X-shaped cross of wood

Saint Andrew thus is cruelly bound.

For two full days our poor saint hangs

and preaches to the gathered crowd.

Twenty thousand hear the tale

of God incarnate spoke aloud.

[Aegeus looks at his watch impatiently. The soldier returns.]

Aegeus: This is the longest sermon I've ever heard in my life.

Soldier: I think he said "in conclusion" about five hours ago.

Aegeus: I'm going to have to reschedule my appointments for the week.

Soldier: The mob is becoming unruly. They demand the release of Saint Andrew.

Aegeus: Mobs, what do *they* know?

Soldier: And your wife told me to tell you that unless you set Saint Andrew free she'll never sleep with you again.

Aegeus: Well, I think he's learned his lesson, don't you? Go cut him down.

Soldier: Right away, sir.

[The soldier leaves. He comes back almost immediately with his arms dangling at his side.]

Aegeus: Well?

Soldier: He said you can't dive halfway into a river, and then my arms went all limp and noodly.

Aegeus: Soldier, I told you to release Saint Andrew!

Soldier: [thwapping Aegeus with loose arms] And I told you, I can't!

[Looking off to where Saint Andrew is, Aegeus and the soldier suddenly shield their eyes.]

Actor: And now a heavenly light is seen,

far brighter than a thousand suns,

obscuring Andrew on the cross

and blinding all the watching ones.

For half an hour the dazzling light

some glory hides from human eyes,

and finally, when the fire has faded,

Saint Andrew breathes his last and dies.

[The Actor solemnly leaves, carrying the X-shaped cross. The soldier exits, leaving Aegeus alone.]

Aegeus: Well, that was unfortunate. But at least it's safe to walk the streets again.

[Aegeus bumps into the devil-dog.]

Aegeus: Hi there, how you doing?

[Aegeus notices the devil tail and picks it up.]

Demon: Don't touch the tail!

[The devil-dog attacks and kills Aegeus, then pants cheerfully at the audience. It drags Aegeus' body off.]

SCENE 6: THE STARTLING CONCLUSION TO OUR TALE

[The Actor enters, followed by Matthias. It is many years later and Matthias is an old man in a large stone church.]

Actor: Now 50 years have come and gone.

Matthias is an elder saint,

retired and living out his days

as bishop of a small church quaint.

Matthias: My life has been quiet and peaceful since Andrew died. I have spent my time maintaining the church begun by those who came before me. And now, before I pass into Heaven, I want to ensure that my beloved church will survive.

[A consultant enters.]

Consultant: Saint Matthias? Good to meet you. I represent Ball and Upstart Research, consultants to the Early Church.

Matthias: [kindly] Thank you for coming.

Consultant: I've been looking at the demographics and it doesn't look good. Your attendance is dropping, your annual givings are down, and your ratings within the general populace are… Well, you're heading toward full-scale fallout within ten years unless you make some drastic changes.

Matthias: Oh dear. What should we do?

Consultant: First, you've got to get your numbers up. More bums in the pews, and, quite frankly, more prosperous bums. You can have the best of intentions, but if you haven't got the funds none of it counts.

Matthias: Oh.

Consultant: What can you do to get more people coming into the church?

Matthias: I hear that Saint Andrew's tomb is very popular; apparently it gives off some sort of a healing oil. People come to visit it from all around. Could we use something like that?

Consultant: My honest opinion? Don't go there. The whole tomb thing implies *death*, which is just too downbeat for today's churchgoer. And the healing, while interesting, might pull in…well, *sick* people, which is really not the clientele we're aiming at.

Matthias: What would you suggest then?

Consultant: The first thing you have to do is figure out what people *want*, and then give it to them. It's a buyer's market for world religions, and you've got to keep a competitive edge if you want to thrive. I've got some graphs and project outlines that you might find interesting.

Matthias: [interested] Graphs, you say.

　　　[There is a loud reverberating knock at the door.]

Matthias: Who could that be?

Consultant: Probably just the wind. Now, let's look at theology. The whole social action angle, it's just not playing in the suburbs.

　　　[Another knock.]

Matthias: Who's there?

Voice from outside the door: Let me in.

Matthias: Who is it?

Voice: A pilgrim.

Consultant: This is a dangerous neighborhood, Saint Matthias. I wouldn't open my door to just anyone.

Matthias: But…

Consultant: Look, let's test him. I'll ask him three questions. If he answers well, we'll let him in. [to person outside] Tell me, pilgrim, what is the most wonderful thing God has ever done in a small space?

Voice: God created the human face. Each is unique, all are different, and in that small circle can be seen all the joy, all the sorrow, all the anger, and all the wisdom that the human race has experienced.

Matthias: Oh, that's a good answer.

Consultant: All right then, pilgrim. Tell me, at what point is the earth higher than the heavens?

Voice: In the person of Jesus Christ, who was flesh, and therefore earth, and now resides at the right hand of our God in heaven.

Matthias: This pilgrim is very smart. We should let him in.

Consultant: No! One more question. Pilgrim, what is the distance from heaven to earth?

[Saint Andrew bursts through the door.]

Andrew: You would know better than I, since you measured it when you fell from heaven into the depths! Matthias, you are being advised by the devil!

[Matthias looks at the Consultant. He pulls a devil tail out from the consultant's jacket.]

Consultant: [taking the tail back] Don't touch the tail.

Andrew: Go back to hell, devil, and do not tempt us anymore.

[The Consultant looks at Andrew for a moment. Finally he shrugs and leaves.]

Matthias: Saint Andrew!?! But you're dead! You've been dead 50 years.

Andrew: What's your point?

Matthias: No point.

Andrew: Good. Come on.

[Andrew starts to stride off.]

Matthias: What? Wait. I'm comfortable now.

Andrew: No time for comfort. We have a job to do.

Matthias: What?

Andrew: We must go to a place called Scotland and build a church.

Matthias: I've never heard of Scotland.

Andrew: It's rocky and cold, with bitter winters, frozen lakes, and hostile barbarians.

Matthias: [sarcastic] Sounds wonderful.

Andrew: Just wait 'til we get to Canada.

Matthias: Let me get my things.

Andrew: No time.

[Andrew strides off, dragging Matthias.]

Matthias: Here we go again.

Andrew: Ever heard of a game called golf?

[Andrew and Matthias leave.]

Actor: And thus the tale of good Saint Andrew,

and of Matthias, his kind friend,

companions on a saintly mission,

has come, dear listeners, to its end.

So peace be with you, gentle folk.

Peace to you, and you, and you.

The peace of Our Lord Jesus Christ,

and of his servant, Saint Andrew.

[The end.]

TABLES TURNED AND THE STONE GETS ROLLED AWAY

An Easter Play (For use with John 20:11–14)

[The following introduction could be printed in a program or order of service: "Easter is not simply a historical event of long ago and far away, it is an experience that is repeated again and again. The characters in this play are biblical followers of Jesus, but they could also be people of our time. Mary might be a woman in her late 20s, possibly with a history of mental illness. Micah could be an aboriginal man who has been unemployed for more than eight years. Esther might be a woman in her 70s who, like 55% of single elderly women in Canada, lives in poverty."

Mary is sitting outside the tomb, weeping. In her arms she holds a balled-up strip of white linen. Micah and Esther approach her. Esther is carrying a large paper shopping bag. Micah taps Mary on the shoulder.]

Micah: Hey, Mary. What are you crying about?

[Mary is surprised and quickly backs away from them.]

Esther: Oh, now, you see? I told you you'd startle her. [to Mary] It's all right, dear. We're friends.

Mary: I'm sorry, do I know you?

Esther: Perhaps not, dear. But we know you.

Micah: Your friends left hours ago. What are you still doing here?

Mary: I don't know. Waiting, I guess?

Micah: Waiting for what?

[Pause.]

Mary: …I don't know.

Esther: [sympathetically] It's been a hard couple of days for you, hasn't it.

Mary: They stole his body, you know. As if it wasn't enough, they had to steal his body, too.

Esther: Indeed. It certainly looks that way.

Mary: It would have been better if I'd never met him. He should have just left me possessed by demons, out of control, without a voice of my own. I mean, what's the use of being shown a world of freedom when, in the end, nothing changes. The poor are still poor. The evil are still evil. And death has the last word. None of it mattered.

[Micah sits down beside Mary.]

Micah: I know what you mean. I used to feel that way too. No money, no job, no family, no nothing. I'd had enough of it all, so I just went blind. I filled my eyes with fog so thick I couldn't see the world around me. I hid myself away in dark corners. But then one day I realized, hey, if nobody sees me, then nobody knows there's a problem. Everyone goes on as if everything's fine. So I dragged and stumbled my way to the temple, 'cause, even though I didn't want to see, I did want to be seen. That way all those temple people would know there's something wrong… That's where your friend found me. He pulled me up on my feet and made me look at the world around me. He showed me that at least one person understood. And that was the start of something.

[Esther sits down on the other side of Mary.]

Esther: My experience was similar. When my dear husband died, oh, so many years ago, he left very little money in the bank. I did my best to manage on a fixed income, but one day, it just ran out. And then I realized that all the money I had in the world, the little bit of cash I had to keep me alive, was just a pittance compared with the expendable profits of the wealthy. So I decided to go down to the temple and put in my two cents, which is practically what it was. Granted, an old woman giving away the last little bit of money she has to live on is a pretty ineffectual protest, and it would have gone totally unnoticed if your friend hadn't been there to point it out. He gave my actions a weight and a dignity they haven't had for many years, and I remember him for that.

Micah: So you see, it *did* matter. It *did* make a difference, at least to us.

Mary: But it's over now. He's dead. And it's all fading so fast. I can't even remember what he looked like. I don't remember anything he said, anything he did. In a little while I'll forget I even knew him at all. And then it'll be over, like it never happened.

Micah: Oh come on, you don't remember Jesus? That can't be true. You've got to remember when he started – all the preaching and the storytelling. Love and compassion and a new world at hand. A new world of justice. Remember that?

Mary: No. I don't remember.

Esther: And how the people heard the stories, but didn't understand, couldn't see what he was trying to show them.

Micah: But that didn't stop Jesus. No siree. He started acting out the stories. He started healing the sick, and casting out demons, and hanging with the "undesirables," and all sorts of miraculous stuff. Remember?

Mary: No.

Esther: And people were intrigued, but still they didn't understand. Didn't see what it meant to them.

Micah: But that didn't stop Jesus. No siree. He went straight to the city. Straight to the center of power. He walked right into the temple and took a stand. You must remember that. It was only a week ago. Remember?

Mary: I told you, I don't remember!

Micah: [gesturing vaguely] You remember. There was this guy? He was…you know, and kind of… He had this, what do you call it? One of those… Oh, come on, you remember.

[Mary looks at him blankly.]

Micah: Esther, give me that cap.

[Esther pulls a visor out of her shopping bag and hands it to Micah.]

Micah: Now come on, you can't tell me you don't remember this guy.

[Micah steps off to the side, puts on the visor, and plays the part of a moneychanger.]

Micah: Pigeons for sale! Get them before they molt. Pigeons for sale! If you can't afford a decent sacrifice, pigeons are the next best thing. Can't do a purification rite without a pigeon. Perfect for the ladies. Get your pigeons here!

Esther: Do you remember him?

Mary: I…don't know.

[As Micah speaks, he sets up an old TV table. He pulls a handful of coins out of his pocket and lays them out on the TV table.]

Micah: Who needs change? Good clean Jewish money for dirty Greek and Roman coins. Remember the rule: If it's got a face, it must be replaced! Can't have idolatrous coinage going into the temple offering. Don't want to offend God with unclean money. And I think you'll find my exchange rates are on par with my competitors. Change here! Who needs change?

Esther: Do you remember, Mary? Do you remember what your friend said?

Mary: I… Maybe?

[Esther takes the cloth out of Mary's hands. She unrolls it and drapes it over Mary's shoulders like a prayer shawl or a stole. She pulls Mary up and sets her before Micah/moneychanger.]

Micah: [continuing his spiel] Going on a trip? Need foreign currency? I'm your man. Good money for bad, bad money for good, whatever you need at competitive rates. [to Mary] Good day, sir.

Mary: [hesitantly] I... I want change. [turning to Esther] That's what he said.

Esther: Indeed.

Mary: I remember now. [to Micah/moneychanger] I want change.

Micah: Very good, sir. And what denominations will we be trading in today?

Mary: What do you charge people for this little service?

Micah: My rates are competitive, sir.

Mary: But you make a profit

Micah: A man has to make a living.

Mary: I see. And your clientele... A lot of poor people?

Micah: Not exclusively.

Mary: But predominantly. And the pigeons?

Micah: Yes, the pigeons are mostly for the poor. And women and lepers. You're not interested in a pigeon, are you?

Mary: How does it feel to be getting rich off the poor?

[Micah, as the moneychanger, looks at Mary warily.]

Micah: I don't get rich, sir, I get by. And those who can't get by, sir, I pity. But if it's God's will that some should go poor, who am I to judge?

Mary: *Whose* will is it that some should go poor?

Micah: God's, sir, of course.

Mary: You lie! Now tell me, why are these people poor?

Micah: [getting angry] It's not my job to ask why these people are poor. It's my job to provide a service. Now, do you want change or not?

Mary: Yes! Yes, I do want change! I want this temple to be a place of refuge for *all* people, like it's supposed to be. I want people like you to stop exploiting the most vulnerable just to make a profit.

Micah: Oh, get off your high horse...

Mary: It was a donkey.

Micah: I don't care what it was. I'm not a greedy profiteer, selling cheap merchandise out of a dark alleyway. I am a legitimate part of the temple economy. I have official sanction and support. Without people like me this temple wouldn't run, and *then* where would your precious poor be? So don't treat me like a criminal, friend. I'm as much a part of this institution as any high priest.

[Mary pauses, slightly taken aback. She looks at Esther, and then back to Micah.]

Mary: So you all work together to gang up on the vulnerable. You help the rulers of the temple oppress the poor, and they help you exploit them for a profit.

Micah: Look, crazy man, I don't know what your problem is. I'm just a guy. A normal guy with a wife and kids. And I'm just trying to do my job.

[Slight pause.]

Mary: [apologetically] You're right. I'm sorry.

[Mary starts to walk away.]

Esther: Is that how it happened, Mary?

[Mary stops. Slight pause. She turns back to the moneychanger.]

Mary: [calmly] No. Not today you're not.

[She takes a corner of the TV table and flips it, sending the coins flying.]

Micah: Hey!! Who do you think you are?!?

Mary: I'm Jesus.

[Esther has put on a large, impressive-looking hat, and now portrays a high priest.]

Esther: What kind of a Jew are you?!? Disrupting the temple and causing a disturbance. Don't you know there are people trying to pray. Have you no respect for religion? No respect for God?

Micah: He's a Galilean, high priest, and you know what that means. You might as well call him an anarchist! All Galileans are alike.

Esther: Is that why you have come here, Jesus? To destroy the establishment, to undermine the government? You know that the temple is the center of the city's economy, and therefore the country's. You know that this is where all the political, cultural, religious, and economic decisions are made. Is that why you're here? To destroy us?

Micah: Round up your gang of cutthroat revolutionaries and get out of here! No wonder he kept talking about the poor. They're all criminals underneath.

Mary: Tell me, high priest, why must people who are poor come to this divided temple, where there is a place for the clean and a place for the unclean? A separate place for men of the right class, shape, and skin color, and another place for women, for slaves, for cripples and lepers, for the poor?

Esther: Every institution has an organizational structure. And, despite what you are trying to imply, the temple is for everyone.

Mary: But why must they come here?

Esther: Why are you asking naive questions? They come because this is where God is. Where else should they go to pay their debts and seek forgiveness?

Mary: Forgiveness for what?

Esther: You know full well for what. For their sins.

Mary: You mean the sin of being poor.

Esther: If there wasn't something *wrong* with them, they wouldn't be poor, would they.

Mary: *That* is why I'm here! To stand against that obscenity! You define some as unclean, as second-class citizens. Then you demand that they make amends for their second-class status. And you both benefit from that arrangement!

[Micah takes a length of string and uses it to measure Mary for a cross, measuring first her height, then her armspan.]

Micah: [sarcastic and threatening] Don't mind me, just taking a few measurements. This should be ready for you by Friday.

Mary: [momentarily unnerved] You're just trying to intimidate me.

Esther: You'd be wise to heed his warning, Jesus.

Mary: No, you'd be wise to heed *my* warning! Your temple economy is based on driving a wedge between the rich and the poor, and the poor end up getting poorer and poorer.

Esther: Are you an economist? …No, I didn't think so. Maybe you should stick to things you know something about. Go back to your preaching about love and morality. People like that. And stop being so rude and disruptive.

Mary: If I was polite and kept in my place, would anything change? Would the temple become what it is supposed to be? According to the Torah, we are to protect the poor, the vulnerable, and the outsiders. The Law calls us to…

Esther: Don't presume to tell me about the Law! I am high priest of the temple. You don't tell me the Law; I tell *you* the Law. Now, you will leave, and you will stop making a nuisance of yourself, or I will be forced to summon a Roman soldier!

Mary: Check the Holy of Holies, high priest! God has leaked out. God has leaked out of the temple and into the streets! God is flowing to lower ground. God is dwelling with the poor, with those who have been labeled unclean, with those who have been blamed for their situation.

Esther: I am warning you, Jesus.

Mary: God has left this place. But God will return. God will return when the temple is once again a place of refuge and justice and compassion for the poor! And that will be a new beginning!

Esther: You know, you're only one man. You can't shut down the business of the temple forever.

Mary: No, but I can shut it down for one day. And one day is enough to start.

Esther: Indeed?

Mary: Indeed!

[Micah and Esther take off their hats and break out of character.]

Micah: You see? You do remember.

Mary: That's what he said! That's what he did. I remember now.

Micah: Of course. How could you forget?

Mary: I remember there was danger. Threats of punishment. Friendly advice to play it safe and keep a low profile.

Micah: But that didn't stop Jesus. No siree. Jesus didn't back down, or run away.

Mary: Because God has anointed me to bring good news to the poor…

Micah: Instead of blaming us for our poverty.

Mary: God has sent me to proclaim release to the captives…

Micah: By treating us, not as second-class citizens, but as people with dignity.

Mary: And recovery of sight to the blind…

Micah: So that no one can say, "It's not *my* problem."

Mary: And to proclaim the year of God's favor.

Micah: When there will be no rich, and there will be no poor, and the only law will be the law of justice and compassion for all God's people.

Esther: Indeed. Which is exactly why they arrested him, and executed him as a criminal to the state, and buried his body in a cold stone tomb.

[Pause. Mary looks at Micah and Esther.]

Mary: [realizing] But that didn't stop Jesus.

Micah: [smiling] No siree.

Mary: Because love is stronger than death. And justice is stronger than oppression.

Esther: And hope is stronger than despair.

Micah: The tables turned, and the stone gets rolled away.

[Mary looks at herself, still wearing the linen cloth draped over her shoulders. She looks up at Esther.]

Mary: And Christ is risen.

Esther: [smiling] Indeed.

Micah: Indeed.

[The end.]

A PRAIRIE NATIVITY

[This play was written to be performed in a barn during the Christmas season. The audience sat on hay bales and had been asked to bring flashlights to provide lighting. On entering the barn, the audience members were each given a tinsel halo to wear.]

PROLOGUE

[The angel Gabriel enters, dressed for cold weather. Gabriel addresses the audience, who represent an angel choir.]

Gabriel: Greetings and blessings, beloved of God. I am Gabriel, the messenger angel, and you are the heavenly host, a choir of angels, singing "Glory to God in the highest." It is almost Christmas, so we must prepare. You might think that we've done this story before, that 2000 years ago it was over and done. But as angels we measure a different time. The Past and Future are always Now, and Now is when our story is told. So Christmas comes, not once, but every year. Not every year, but every hour. Not every hour, but every minute, every second, every moment, every time that Love is born. Two thousand years ago is Now. Far Away is Here. Our story is about to begin.

Our story says that the glory of God shone around, so those of you who have flashlights, especially any young angels in the group, can help by directing your light at the ones who are speaking.

The story will take us to a place called Bethlehem. The name means "House of Bread." It is a place where wheat is grown, a farming community. But as I said, this story takes place in the Here and Now. We'll find this Bethlehem in the middle of prairie winter. No palm trees, no desert, no camels. Just snow, and wind, some barnyard cats, and a great wide sky overhead. If angels would survive in this clime, certain adaptations must be made. Feathery wings will be turned in for down-filled coats. Dazzling white robes can be replaced by a pair of warm long-johns. Our harps can be left behind in favor of warm mitts and a toque. To any observer we will appear as natural inhabitants of this snowy world. Only our angelic voices and heavenly harmonies will reveal our true natures. Let us practice as an angel choir…

Gabriel: [sings] See amid the winter's snow,

> born for us on earth below,

> see, the tender Lamb appears,

> promised from eternal years.*

Angel Choir: [sings] Hail, thou ever blessed morn;

> hail, redemption's happy dawn;

* Words to "See amid the winter's snow" by Edward Caswall (1814–1878)

sing through all Jerusalem,

Christ is born in Bethlehem.

SCENE 1

Gabriel: Let those with light reveal me, Gabriel, the messenger of God, and I will start the story… Humans are a puzzling lot. We angels find them strange. By our counting they were made a minute and a half ago, and yet have spent an eternity in longing. It is as if they were born with a God-shaped hole in their heart. They live in hope and in fear, and only a few know what it is they yearn for. They are an odd creation – sometimes sleepy, sometimes crazy. We don't claim to understand them. But God does. God knows them and knows their longing. And now, after a minute and half of eternity, God will respond. And so I am sent, to a girl named Mary.

   [Mary enters.]

Gabriel: Hail, Mary, full of grace!

Mary: Um, hi.

Gabriel: The Lord our God is with thee, and thou art most highly favored.

Mary: I don't know you, do I?

Gabriel: I have been sent with a message for you.

Mary: Oh yeah? Who from?

Gabriel: From God.

Mary: OK, whoever you are, you're creeping me out. I'm going to go inside now.

Gabriel: Don't be afraid, Mary. I am bringing good news. God has heard the prayers of the people. God longs to be with the people in the place that they live.

Mary: Are you a minister or something?

Gabriel: I'm an angel.

Mary: You don't look like an angel.

Gabriel: I'm sort of in disguise.

Mary: Why would an angel have to go in disguise?

Gabriel: I know about you humans. I know how they treat things that are foreign and strange. It is safer for me to go in disguise.

Mary: So God wants to be with the people. What does that have to do with me?

Gabriel: You will have a baby, who will be a symbol of Hope and Justice and Compassion. This child will be an important person – a teacher, a preacher, a healer, a leader. Your baby will be called a child of God.

Mary: That all sounds really nice, but I'm not married.

Gabriel: Are you suggesting that women in this world never get pregnant before they're married?

Mary: Well, no.

Gabriel: Your child will be a child of the Holy Spirit, and you will be the Mother of God.

Mary: But I can't get pregnant. My mom would kill me.

Gabriel: Everything will be fine. God has chosen you.

Mary: This isn't how I planned things. I was going to go to Europe, maybe get a job, and then some day, eventually, *maybe* get married, and have a kid or two. But not now. I mean, I'm not even finished school yet!

Gabriel: Don't be afraid, Mary.

Mary: You should go and look up my friend Allison. She's got no plans for the rest of her life.

Gabriel: Your child will be God, and God will be with us, and everything you see will be holy and special. And you will name the child "Salvation."

Mary: You already know the baby's name?

Gabriel: Yes.

Mary: I suppose you're going to tell me the sex too.

Gabriel: Do you want to know.

Mary: Might as well.

Gabriel: A boy.

Mary: A boy. Named Salvation?

Gabriel: Salvation.

Mary: He's going to get teased at school.

Gabriel: All will be well, Mary… Oh, and by the way, your second cousin Elizabeth from Amaranth* is also pregnant.

* Feel free to replace "Amaranth" with the name of a nearby town known to the audience.

Mary: Yeah, right. She's, like, 93!

[Gabriel nods.]

Mary: Weird.

Gabriel: God bless thee and fare thee well. [to angels] These affairs are not easily arranged. It is not by habit that Christmas happens every year, but by miracle and luck.

[Gabriel leaves. Mary sits on a hay bale and muses to herself.]

Mary: Wow.

A fluttering of wings, like pigeons in the hay loft.

And a fluttering in my heart.

My heart is beating like a steam engine, banging against my rib cage.

My heart is singing.

What a surprising thing for a heart to do.

My heart is singing that God is real, and great, and good.

I look around and see angels everywhere.

Every tree, and star, and snowflake is filled with God.

Every sound and smell and touch is filled with God.

And everything that isn't real,

everything that doesn't give life, that pushes some down,

that stands in the way,

everything that is not real

falls away,

and only God is seen

in a blaze of Green Life and Justice.

Amen, and let it be.

[Mary leaves. Gabriel enters.]

SCENE 2

Gabriel: In the Now and in the Here nine months have passed. Gentle Mary has given birth to her firstborn son, the Holy Child, in the place called Bethlehem, the House of Bread. And so we go to find her and the Christ child to offer our thanks and to sing our praises…

Gabriel: [sings] Lo, within a manger lies

God, who built the starry skies,

who enthroned in height sublime

sits amid the cherubim.

Angel Choir: [sings] Hail, thou ever blessed morn;

hail, redemption's happy dawn;

sing through all Jerusalem,

Christ is born in Bethlehem.

[Mary enters.]

Gabriel: Hail, Mary, full of grace!

Mary: You didn't tell me I'd be giving birth in a barn!

Gabriel: The child is born?

Mary: Yes, no help from you! I've got him wrapped up as warmly as I can and sleeping in a feed trough.

Gabriel: Wasn't there some other place you could stay?

Mary: You didn't give me any money, which rules out the hotel. And nobody else around here has room for us. It's the holidays, in case you've forgotten.

Gabriel: Didn't you tell them that you were giving birth to the Son of God?

Mary: Yeah, that went over really well. If this little guy is going to be somebody important, he's off to a pretty strange start.

Gabriel: All will be well, Mary.

Mary: You keep saying that.

Gabriel: Do you doubt it?

Mary: …No. But I still could use some company.

Gabriel: Fear not. We, the heavenly host, will spread the word of the Christ-child's birth.

[Mary leaves.]

Gabriel: And as the story goes, there were in that region shepherds, who lived in the fields, watching their flocks by night.

[Two farmers enter.]

Farmer 1: Cold night.

Farmer 2: Very cold.

Farmer 1: Got to be pushing minus 30.

Farmer 2: You think?

Farmer 1: Sure.

Farmer 2: That's cold.

Farmer 1: Cold night for farming.

Farmer 2: You can say that again.

Farmer 1: Cold night for farming.

Farmer 2: Yup.

[Waitress enters with a coffeepot.]

Waitress: You boys ready for some more coffee?

Farmer 1: Thanks, Jenny.

Farmer 2: Thank you.

[She fills their cups.]

Farmer 1: Yup, cold night out there.

Farmer 2: Got any more of those donuts back there, Jenny?

Waitress: I'll check.

Farmer 2: Sure is coming down out there.

Farmer 1: Wouldn't want to be outside on a night like tonight.

Farmer 2: No sir.

Farmer 1: A lot of brass monkeys singing soprano tonight.

Farmer 2: I think the wind's letting up a little.

Farmer 1: You think?

Farmer 2: No, I guess not… Say, Jake. You ever see one of those crop circles?

Farmer 1: What, you mean those ones that are supposed to be made by flying saucers?

Farmer 2: Yeah, those ones.

Farmer 1: Nope, never seen one.

Farmer 2: I think maybe I saw one over at the schoolyard the other day. Not a crop circle, mind you, because there's no crop on the schoolyard. But in the snow, you know, this big circle.

[Farmer 1 looks at Farmer 2. Slight pause.]

Farmer 1: That's the kids, Dwayne. They go out at recess and they run around in a circle.

Farmer 2: Oh.

Farmer 1: Why? Did you think it was from a flying saucer?

Farmer 2: Well, I didn't know. I just thought it was kind of odd.

Farmer 1: You didn't notice the footprints coming from and going to the circle?

Farmer 2: Well, I thought maybe that's where the aliens came out of their spacecraft to look around before going back in because it was too cold.

Farmer 1: You been drinking that purple gas again, Dwayne? I told you, that's just for the machinery.

Farmer 2: Come on, Jake, don't you think maybe there's more to the universe than just us? Have you ever thought about the possibility of intelligent life on other planets?

Farmer 1: At the moment, I'm not so sure there's intelligent life on *this* planet.

[Gabriel enters.]

Gabriel: Don't be afraid!

Farmer 1: Why should we be afraid?

Gabriel: I am an angel of the Lord.

Farmer 1: You don't look like an angel.

Gabriel: Yeah, well you don't look like shepherds; get over it. I bring you news of great joy, and joy to be shared by all the people. Today, in this place where you live, a child has been born.

Farmer 1: Well, that's nice.

Gabriel: This child is Christ the Lord.

Farmer 1: Is that his first name or his last name?

Gabriel: He is the Christ. The Human One. The one who lives and acts as God would. The personification of God's love and compassion for all of creation. A savior for the people. He will make the world a better place.

Farmer 1: Really? That's great. Is he going to give us a longer growing season?

Gabriel: Well, no.

Farmer 2: Better prices on our wheat?

Gabriel: No.

Farmer 1: Can he at least get us a good deal on our herbicide for next season?

Gabriel: I don't think so.

Farmer 1: So, in what way exactly is he going to make the world a better place for us?

Gabriel: This child is Hope, and the knowledge that you are not alone. And this will be a sign: you will find the baby, wrapped up warm against the wind, and lying in a feed trough.

[Gabriel leaves.]

Farmer 2: Should we go, Jake?

Farmer 1: Oh, probably. Maybe I'll just have another cup of coffee and wait for the wind to die down a bit.

Waitress: I don't believe you two! An angel just walked in here and told you that Christ has been born, right now, right here! You ought to be out the door running, trying to find that child.

Farmer 1: We're going.

Waitress: Then GO!

Farmer 1: OK, OK! …I guess that means we're not getting any coffee, eh?

Farmer 2: Wait a minute. Do you hear that? It sounds like a throng of the heavenly host, singing Glory to God in the highest…

Gabriel: [sings] Say, ye holy shepherds, say

what your joyful news today;

wherefore have ye left your sheep

on a lonely mountain steep?

Angel Choir: [sings] Hail, thou ever blessed morn;

hail, redemption's happy dawn;

sing through all Jerusalem,

Christ is born in Bethlehem.

[The Farmers and the Waitress leave.]

SCENE 3

Gabriel: So they hurried away and found Mary, and the baby lying in the manger. When they saw the child they repeated what they had been told about him, and everyone who heard it was astonished at what the shepherds had to say.

[The Farmers and the Waitress enter.]

Waitress: What a beautiful baby.

Farmer 2: All babies are beautiful.

Farmer 1: I wish I had more money. I could have brought a nice present.

Waitress: I brought a cherry pie, and a thermos of coffee to keep them both warm, and to remind them of hospitality.

Farmer 2: I brought him a horse blanket and a bag of birdseed. Maybe the seed will attract some chickadees who will entertain him with their chirping, and remind him that beauty can still thrive in the cold and snow.

Farmer 1: Maybe I ought to run out and buy something.

Waitress: It's December 25th. You'll never find anything open.

Farmer 1: Wait! I'll give him this ball. My father gave it to me when I was a boy, his father gave it to him, and his father gave it to him. It's good for children to play and have fun, and maybe it will remind him of tradition.

[The Farmers and the Waitress go in to the stable.]

Gabriel: Once again, for the first time, the story has been told, and we, the heavenly host, can make our way back to our heavenly home to warm ourselves from this wintry world. Come, angel choir, let us fly.

Mary: Wait a minute! That's it? You leave me with this baby and then, "Bye bye, so long, God bless," and trundle off back to heaven?!? How am I supposed to raise this child to be the Christ alone?

Gabriel: I thought you would know how to do that.

Mary: Why would I know how to do that? Have you ever heard the expression: "It takes a village to raise a child"? Don't you suppose that might apply to the Christ child as well?

Gabriel: You have the…shepherds.

Mary: They're great and all, but there's only three of them. We're going to need more community than that.

Gabriel: You are full of wisdom as well as grace, Mary. [to the choir] Angel choir, your duties have been extended and expanded. You will continue as you are, like people of this time and place. No longer a heavenly choir, but a community of friends. And as angels in disguise you will be godparents to this child, in every form hereafter born. You are called to nurture this child. This child who is Hope. This child who is Peace. This child who is God-among-us, here and now. Do not let Hope weaken or starve for lack of attention.

EPILOGUE

Gabriel: So Mary treasured these things and pondered them in her heart. And the choir of angels became a community, and the community an angel choir. Humans are a puzzling lot, born with a God-shaped hole in their heart. But on a cold winter's night, in the Right Here and Now, we might feel that hole filled up and made full, by the birth of a child, by the presence of Hope, by the song of hearts in harmony with God's creation.

Gabriel: [sings] Sacred infant, all divine,

what a mighty love was thine,

thus to come from highest bliss

down to such a world as this!

Angel Choir: [sings] Hail, thou ever blessed morn;

hail, redemption's happy dawn;

sing through all Jerusalem,

Christ is born in Bethlehem.

[The end.]

MAYBE ONE?

A theatrical history of the United Church

SCENE 1: IN THE BEGINNING

[Darkness.]

Actor 1: In the beginning there was nothing. And God said, "Let there be light."

[Lights come up to reveal two actors on stage.]

Actor 2: So. "A theatrical history of the United Church." Where do we start?

Actor 1: You've read the script, haven't you?

Actor 2: Of course I've…*skimmed* it.

Actor 1: Then you know that where we start is at the beginning.

Actor 2: Ah, a very good place to start. [to audience] In the beginning. 1925. A historic ceremony in Toronto's Mutual Street Arena…

Actor 1: Um…

Actor 2: What?

Actor 1: That's not the beginning.

Actor 2: Oh… OK. In the beginning. The early 20th century. Social change, immigration, a world war, western expansion…

[Actor 1 clears his/her throat. Actor 2 looks and realizes that that isn't the beginning either.]

Actor 2: Ah, right. In the beginning, there were Presbyterians, and Methodists, and Congregationalists…

[Actor 1 shakes his/her head. Actor 2 gives it another shot.]

Actor 2: In the beginning, there was a land! And a people. Who were joined by Christians from across the sea…

Actor 1: Sorry.

Actor 2: [trying even harder] In the beginning was the Protestant Reformation. No! The Catholic church – No, no, no!! The early Christian community!

Actor 1: In the beginning was the Word. And the Word was with God, and the Word was God. And the Word said, "As you sent me into the world, I have sent them into the world. That all may be one."

Actor 2: Maybe one?

Actor 1: Maybe one.

Actor 2: ...I think you could have *told* me that was the beginning.

Actor 1: You should have read your script.

[They start to leave the stage.]

Actor 2: [on the way out] Now 1925?

Actor 1: Now 1925.

SCENE 2: UNION NIGHT IN CANADA

[A hockey arena. Music: *Hockey Night in Canada* theme. Two sportscasters enter. Ron McCain wears an orange CBC blazer. Dawn Sherry wears a high-collared shirt and a plaid tie, and speaks in a loud, obnoxious voice.]

Ron: Good evening, church fans, and welcome to "Union Night in Canada," from the Mutual Street Arena in Toronto. I'm Ron McCain, and as usual, I'm here with the ebullient and sophisticated Dawn Sherry.

Dawn: It's gonna be one heckuva rock'em, sock'em game.

Ron: It certainly will, Dawn, as the Methodists, Presbyterians, and Congregationalists all try to unite into one amalgamated, consolidated, confederated, combined...

Dawn: Look, McCain, stop trying to be Howard Cossell. Why don't you just say "united" and get it over with?

Ron: All right, Dawn, I will. One "united" church. The date is June 10, 1925. Plans for church union have been in the works since 1902, but it all comes down to this moment, this ceremony, this arena – Mutual Street Arena, Toronto, Ontario, Canada. It's a packed house here. There are 7046 people in the crowd, a choir of 250 representing all three denominations, 350 commissioners, three of whom are women. There are representatives of the so-called "Union Churches" coming from...

Dawn: Yeah, yeah, like anybody cares. Let's get to the fighting.

Ron: There certainly has been fighting, Dawn. The Church Union team is going to have to play the best game of their season if they want to see this United Church idea get off the ground.

Dawn: Let me say a thing about this here Church Union. Out in the west, they been doin' the "union" thing for years. 'Cuz it's *practical*, and it's an *effective* way to keep up with the changin' society.

Ron: So in your opinion Church Union is pretty much inevitable?

Dawn: In your dreams, McCain. That Anti-Union team is a buncha heavy-hitters. They're gonna take it to the boards tryin' to stop Church Union.

> [The Church-Union and Anti-Union teams "skate" in, wearing a combination of ecclesiastic garb and hockey equipment.]

Ron: And here come the teams! Reverend George Pidgeon of the Church-Union team will be facing off against Reverend Ephraim Scott on the Anti-Union team.

Dawn: That Pidgeon guy's a good player. It ain't no wonder they named him moderator of Presbyterian Church. He may be named after a bird, but he ain't no chicken.

Ron: What do you think about Ephraim Scott, captain of the Anti-Union team, Dawn?

Dawn: Ephraim Scott, now this guy's a bruiser. As the editor of the Presbyterian Record, he puts the "tank" in cantankerous. Some people say he's too old, but I say at 80 he's just coming into his prime. I mean, look at Wayne Gretzky. He was 99 when he retired.

Ron: That was his number, Dawn, not his age.

> [Pidgeon and Scott stand on opposite sides of the "ice."]

Ron: It looks like Pidgeon and Scott are in position and we're moments away from the faceoff!

Dawn: Presbyterian meets Presbyterian. We're gonna see some sparks here.

> [The referee blows a whistle and Pidgeon and Scott "skate" toward each other. Pidgeon holds out his hand for a handshake, Scott moves to take it…]

Ron: There's the hand, and…

> [Scott quickly veers off and moves away, leaving Pidgeon with his hand out.]

Ron: Oh, a snub!! A definite snub! Let's see that again.

> [Pidgeon and Scott re-enact the offer and refusal of the handshake in slow-motion. Scott moves off to the side, where he is joined by Dawn.]

Dawn: All right, listen up, I'm here at ice-level with the Reverend Ephraim Scott. Eph, that was some move there.

Scott: [furious] I willna shake hands with that man. This union is a national crrime! They arre trrying to blot oot the Prresbyterian Churrch! But we'll stop them. Aye, we've a strrong defense, but, mark my words, we can be offensive as well.

[Chown, the captain of the Church-Union team, joins Dawn.]

Dawn: OK, I've also got Dr. Samuel Chown here, General Superintendent of the Methodist Church, and captain of the Church-Union team. How about the beating Pidgeon took in that faceoff, Sam?

Chown: It's not over 'til it's over, Dawn. We're inspired. We have a vision of dominion-wide service. We're going to give it 110% and be a unified force for bringing Christ's message into the world.

Dawn: That's great, Sam. Didn't you once say that the reason you was doin' all this was to keep the Catholics from gaining religious control of the country?

Chown: Well, uh, um...

Dawn: Come on, Sam, don't try weaseling out.

[In a corner of the "ice" a scuffle breaks out, eventually drawing in all the players. Scenes of roughing, high-sticking, pushing into the boards.]

Ron: Sorry to interrupt, Dawn, but things are really heating up at center ice! One of the Anti-Union players has just been sent to the penalty box for trying to coerce another player into voting against union. A brawl has erupted and the referees seem helpless to control it.

[Two players drop their gloves and go at each other. Much pushing and shoving. Angry shouts of "Methodist!" "Presbyterian!" and "Congregationalist!"]

Ron: [shouting over the noise] It's pandemonium down there, folks! I can't hear myself think!

Dawn: Now *that's* the way the game should be played!

[Scott and perhaps another Anti-Union player leave, shaking their fists.]

Ron: Oh, and it looks like 38% of the Presbyterians are opting out of union. The Presbyterians are split!

Dawn: That's gotta hurt! They're heading to the showers and they're taking Knox College with them!

Ron: Hang on, Dawn. Something's happening at center ice. Apparently the Congregationalists, the Methodists, and the remaining Presbyterians are trying to make a go at it.

[The battered players fall into a huddle. Music: Arena organ playing the "Charge!" theme.]

Ron: It looks like… It looks like…

[The players lift their sticks to form a pinnacle, and cheer.]

Ron: Yes!! A union! A definite union! Kind of grumpy, and not too happy about all the splits in the respective congregations, but a union nonetheless. The only thing left now is the closing hymn.

Dawn: The Congregationalists are pushing for *God of Grace and God of Glory*; the Presbyterians want something from the Scottish Psalter; and the Methodists are insisting on something by Wesley.

[The players smile as they politely discuss. Suddenly two players drop their gloves and go at each other.]

Ron: Let's just leave them to work that out while we announce the most valuable player of the union. The game's MVP will become the new church's first moderator.

Dawn: What, no car?

Ron: No car. So who's your guess, Dawn?

Dawn: I gotta say Chown. He played a solid game, and though I think he coulda dropped the gloves a little sooner, he really held that team together.

Ron: Chown's my choice. too. But I don't think the demoralized Presbyterians are going to like the idea of a Methodist moderator. That's bound to cause some hurt feelings.

[Chown rises.]

Ron: Chown's on his feet, presumably accepting nomination.

Chown: I've thought it over and I feel a Presbyterian should be nominated moderator. I'd like one vote cast for George Campbell Pidgeon.

[The players begin to sing *The Church's One Foundation*, as they lift Pidgeon up and carry him off the ice.]

Dawn: Now that's a classy move. Chown was a shoe-in for moderator, but he passed it up for church unity.

Ron: And George Pidgeon is the new moderator of the new United Church! What a historic day, Dawn! An exciting bit of denominational union and an act of real love that certainly bodes well for this new church. That's the game, folks. Thanks for tuning in. Tune in again in 1968 for another exciting game of "Union Night in Canada." Local blackouts in effect.

[Dawn and Ron leave.]

SCENE 3: BASIS OF UNION COUNTDOWN

[A middle-aged radio D.J. enters, picking up in the middle of a show.]

Casem: Hi, I'm U. C. Casem, and this is the Basis of Union Countdown. We've been counting down the top 20 Articles of Faith in the United Church Basis of Union, from number 20… to number 1. We're about to announce the Article of Faith sitting in the number 1 spot this week. The name of that article – in a minute; but first, little Susie Farquhar, from Dusty Knee, Saskatchewan, writes in to say, "U. C., I love your show. I listen to it every week. But I find myself disagreeing with many of the articles that make it into the top 20. Should I quit the church?"

Well, Susie, the theology of the United Church, as summarized in the 20 Articles of Faith, comes from two very different streams. The Calvinist theology of the Presbyterians and the Congregationalists is, at times, almost irreconcilable with the Wesleyan theology of the Methodists. Think of it as like trying to make a band combining the Beach Boys and the Supremes. So it's not surprising you have trouble with some of the articles. Many people do. That's why ministers only have to be in *essential* agreement with the Basis of Union, but in *total* agreement with the pension plan. Thanks for writing in, Susie, and now, the number 1 article in the 20 Articles of Faith…

Sitting tight at number 1, the spot it's held since the Basis of Union was written, Article number 1, *Of God*. "We believe in the one only living and true God, a Spirit, infinite, eternal and unchangeable; plenteous in mercy, full of compassion, and abundant in goodness and truth." Article 1, Of God.

Well, that's the Basis of Union Countdown for this week. I'm U. C. Casem, and until next time, keep watching that faith.

[U.C. Casem leaves.]

SCENE 4: CONTROVERSY!

[Ms. Earnestine Curmudgeon, a prim and proper gentlewoman enters. (She is occasionally played by a man, but doesn't need to be.) She is carrying a small blue hymnbook. She is clearly upset.]

Curmudgeon: I told them – long before we got into this whole union shambles – I said to the women of the Ladies Auxiliary, "Ladies, beware. The traditions of our forefathers will be deserted and we will be left desolate."

And sure enough, my words have come true. The camel's spine has been shattered and *this* is the offending straw, the cancer in the bud, the splinter in the eye of all faithful Christians… This new hymnary!

They say we need a new hymnbook to reflect our three denominations. Does this mean maliciously omitting those beautiful songs that form the cornerstone of our religious life? Where is *Bringing in the Sheaves!*? Where is *Amazing Grace!*? Where is *The Church in the Wildwood!*? [singing, poorly] "Oh come, come, come, come, come to the church in the wildwood…" How could they leave out those songs? And the songs they *have* included – unsingable!

I am angry. I am very angry. I cannot stand idly by and watch my faith, which I hold so dear – pardon my language, but – *pee-ed* on in such a way. I won't stand for it. I can't stand for it. I'm leaving the church. This is the last you'll see of me!

[Curmudgeon storms off.]

SCENE 5: THE PUNCH AND NELLIE SHOW

[Punch, of the Punch and Judy puppet plays, enters, complete with soft "whacker stick." Punch elicits response from the audience.]

Punch: Hey boys and girls, are you ready for another Punch and Judy show? Eh? Eh? I bet you are. I am the lovable and ever-popular, Mr. Punch! YAY!! My nagging wife, Judy, will be coming on in a minute, but first, let me tell you what she's been pestering me about lately. Judy seems to think that women should be allowed to be ministers in the United Church. Isn't that silly? What do you think I should tell her, boys and girls? Should we say that women can be ordained? No! We're going to say, [singing] "No, nay, never! – whack, whack, whack, whack! – No, nay, never, no sir, will you *be* a min-ister. No, never, no way!" We're ready for her nagging now, aren't we, boys and girls. Oh, shh, here comes Judy.

Voice-over: For today's performance, the role of Judy will be played by Ms. Nellie McClung.

Punch: Oh oh.

[Enter Nellie McClung, as Judy.]

Nellie: Good afternoon, Mr. Punch.

Punch: Judy, my darling, lovely, [aside] *nagging*, [and back to Judy] wife. How are you?

Nellie: I'll be considerably better when you smarten up and realize that women can be just as competent in ordained ministry as men, and in some cases, more.

Punch: [aside] She doesn't waste any time, does she.

Nellie: I hereby submit a resolution to the 1928 General Council, calling for the ordination of women.

Punch: Ordain women? Well, let me think about it. OK, I've thought about it. The answer is "No, nay, never! – Wha-…

[Nellie gingerly takes Punch's whacker stick and tosses it away.]

Punch: Well…ahem, I guess we'll have to try a different approach.

Nellie: The floor is open for debate.

Punch: [addressing the audience in high rhetoric] Boys and girls of the General Council, what the church needs at present is not more femininity, but more masculinity. Will the work of the church be made more attractive to strong virile manhood by the proposed ordination of women to the ministry?

Nellie: Let me get this straight, Mr. Punch. Women can help pay off mortgages, or build churches, or any other *light* work, but the *real* work of the church, such as moving *resolutions* in the general conferences or assemblies, must be done by strong, hardy men.

Punch: [addressing the audience] Boys and girls, ordination for women must be opposed, because: A) There is no precedent in church history…

Nellie: Translation – "Well, we never heard of such a thing."

Punch: B) Most women don't want it…

Nellie: Translation – "Your sisters might not be pleased."

Punch: And C) It would not be accepted by other churches…

Nellie: Translation – "What would the Joneses say?!"

Punch: Boys and girls, vote no.

Nellie: Let's put it to the vote. All in favor? All opposed?

[Nellie and Punch do a quick count.]

Nellie: 76 for. 26 against. The motion is carried.

[Punch looks at Nellie sheepishly.]

Punch: [à la Cary Grant] Judy, Judy, Judy.

Nellie: November 4, 1936; Lydia Gruchy is ordained as a minister of United Church of Canada – the first woman ever.

[Nellie tweaks Punch's nose, smiles, and leaves.]

Punch: There was a time when a Scottish preacher could pray, "Lord, we thank thee that God created women to make men comfortable." He cannot pray that way now.

[Punch sighs and fades away.]

SCENE 6: THE DEPRESSION

[A dejected man enters, cap in hand. He speaks to the audience as if speaking to a psychiatrist.]

Patient: Thanks for seeing me, doc. It's this depression. I can't seem to shake it. Ever since the stock market crash of '29. And then the prairies turned into a dust bowl… I lost my job; I couldn't support my family. I started hopping on boxcars, going from town to town, looking for work. But there is no work. It's awful, doc! I mean, if it wasn't for those nice United Church women running the soup kitchen out of the church basement, I don't know how I could have made it this far… I heard there were some United Church people lobbying the government to do things like regulate banking, but they got labeled as communists, and nobody listened. It's all so…depressing! You've got to help me, doc! How am I going to get out of this depression?

[The patient freezes and remains on stage.]

SCENE 7: THE FEARLESS MIDGET

[A World War II army chaplain enters, wearing a uniform and clerical collar. He speaks to the audience, as if writing a letter home.]

Chaplain: Dear Doris,

War. I can't begin to describe its awfulness. The men seem to appreciate my presence here as a chaplain; I've even earned a nickname – "the fearless midget." I don't know why – I'm not a midget, after all, and I'm far from fearless. Yes, I did go back to retrieve a wounded man and ended up capturing six Germans in the process, but that was more luck than bravery.

Thank you for sending a copy of the "Witness Against the War" document. Those 68 United Church ministers may be right; war *is* an abomination. But we are in a battle against evil itself and I think their "witness" is out of place! We don't need criticism; we need prayers, and plenty of them. If a stray bullet should find its way to me, I want it said that I fought the good fight.

Your loving, but far from fearless, husband, Arthur.

[The chaplain freezes, and remains on stage.]

SCENE 8: INTERNMENT

[Tak Komiyama, a Japanese-Canadian minister, enters.]

Tak: Green tea slowly sipped

I stare through the barbed wire fence

Waiting to go home

Tak Komiyama

United Church minister

Nineteen forty-two

Born in Canada

But born with almond-shaped eyes

And therefore suspect

All my precious books

Taken. The notes I had made

In the margins lost

If we had been spies

We would have seen this coming.

Instead, here we are.

[The patient from the Depression scene speaks, representing the United Church.]

Patient: The United Church wishes to disassociate itself from vicious and unchristian attitudes, and holds fast to the faith that in Christ there is no distinction of race and color. We will support the relocated Japanese-Canadians with food, supplies, lodging, and education.

Tak: Four years of waiting

The tea is too cold to drink

Nineteen forty-five

Chaplain: May eighth, V-E Day

It is the end of the war

Soon we will go home

Tak: Then Hiroshima

It is the end of the world

What does "home" mean now?

[The patient, the chaplain, and Tak all slowly leave.]

SCENE 9: THE ENDICOTT ZONE

Narrator: [à la Rod Serling] The Boom… Imagine, if you will, the 1950s in Canada. The war is over, the economy is picking up, the population is growing, and new churches are being built to keep up. It is a boom period for the country and for the United Church.

[A stereotypical 1950s TV father-figure enters and greets his stereotypical 1950s TV family. All smiles.]

Dad: Hi, honey, I'm home.

Mom: Ward! How was work?

Dad: Oh, you know, same old same old.

Daughter: Daddy!

Dad: Princess! How was school today?

Daughter: It was great! Lance Whitebread asked me to the senior prom!

Dad: Did you check with your mother?

Daughter: She says it's all right.

Dad: That's great then.

Daughter: And Timmy qualified for the varsity basketball team.

Dad: Well, Timmy, I'm very proud of you.

[The father gives the son a firm handshake.]

Son: Thanks, Dad.

Dad: So, what say we have a barbecue to celebrate?

Mom: Well, I have been preparing a roast all day, but I suppose we can use it for sandwiches tomorrow.

[The daughter brings Dad his apron, a spatula, and perhaps a chef's hat. Dad fires up the barbecue. The neighbor, Reverend Bob, leans over the fence.]

Rev. Bob: Say there, neighbor.

Dad: Say there, Reverend Bob. Are you joining us? I'm cooking up some steaks.

Rev. Bob: Steaks, you say? Well, don't mind if I do.

Dad: [satisfied] Good neighbors, good family, good job, good barbecue. Life is good.

Narrator: Nothing, it seems, could disturb the 1950s euphoria.

Dad: Nothing, it seems, could disturb this 1950s euphoria.

[Reverend James Endicott stumbles in, exhausted and panting as if having run a great distance. Everyone stops to look at him.]

Endicott: [panting] To External Affairs minister Lester Pearson, stop. From Reverend James Endicott, United Church missionary in China, 1952, stop. Personal investigations reveal undeniable evidence of large-scale continuing American germ warfare on Chinese mainland, stop.

Dad: [trying to ignore Endicott] June, I think we're just about ready for the steaks.

Daughter: Daddy, who's that man?

Dad: That's the son of the United Church's second moderator, princess. Don't pay any attention to him.

Endicott: American germ warfare on Chinese mainland. Urge you protest shameful violation of United Nations agreement. Stop.

Mom: Oh dear.

Dad: Look, everyone, we're having a pleasant family barbecue! Just ignore him and he'll go away.

Endicott: Germ warfare in China and Korea. This can be confirmed by North Korean and Chinese officials.

Mom: Who wants Jello One-Two-Three?

Daughter: [frightened] Daddy?

Narrator: Imagine, if you will, the 1950s in Canada: the Cold War and paranoid anti-communism.

Endicott: Urge you protest…

Dad: [turning on Endicott] Now look here, you commie stooge, stop spreading these damnable lies. Why don't you go back to the Kremlin where you belong!

Endicott: We have to speak out…

Dad: Reverend Bob, he's one of yours; can't you do something about him?

Rev. Bob: Now, Endicott, we wish you'd stop saying such things. You know it's not true.

Daughter: America wouldn't do that, would they, Daddy?

Dad: You're supposed to be a minister of the gospel, not some red propagandist. Who's pulling your strings, Endicott? How much are your Moscow masters paying you to spew these treasonous lies?

[Everyone starts to surround Endicott. Dad threatens him with the spatula.]

Son: Commie!

Mom: Judas!

Rev. Bob: Liar!

Dad: Phony! If this is the price of free speech, it's too high for me!

Son: Red!

All: Red! Red! Red!

[Everyone circles Endicott, chanting "Red." The chanting shifts into barking and growling. Endicott raises his arms to protect himself. Everyone freezes.]

Narrator: The media savaged Endicott and hounded his family. The United Church, caught up like the rest of Canada in the Red Scare, repudiated Endicott's claims and left him to the wolves.

[The threatening actors let out a wolf howl, and then disperse. Music: *Twilight Zone* theme.]

Narrator: To speak out and risk condemnation, or to stay silent. A constant dilemma for people of faith, and for the United Church… Thirty years later, the church apologized for their treatment of Endicott.

SCENE 10: NEW CURRICULUM

[A new narrator enters, holding a 1960s Sunday school textbook.]

Narrator: In the early '60s, the United Church put out study programs for adults and for Sunday schools, using the kind of biblical scholarship and interpretation that had been taught in theological schools and seminaries for years but was now, for the first time, reaching people in the pews.

[Ms. Curmudgeon storms in, prim, proper, and mad as ever.]

Curmudgeon: Myth!? Myth, they say! ...*Apparently* the world was *not* created in seven days, despite the fact that the Bible clearly says it was! Noah and the flood. Jonah and the whale. The entire Christian faith, reduced to myths and lies by these new curriculum blasphemers and their atheistic philosophy! No virgin birth?! Why, it is the same as saying that Christ was not divine. For this they spent a million dollars?! These books should all be gathered in one spot and burned! If I weren't a Christian woman I might go so far as to say the *authors* of these books should be burned as well. But I *am* a Christian woman. And I will rest calm in the knowledge that these godless deceivers will find certain destruction at the hands of the Creator they defy. Mark my words, this new curriculum is a wholesale sell-out to Satan. I won't stand for it. I can't stand for it. I'm leaving the church. This is the last you'll see of me!

[She storms out.]

SCENE 11: ANGLICAN TANGO

[An actor illustrates the "Here is the church, here is the steeple" hand game.]

Actor: Here is the church.

Here is the steeple.

Open the doors, and...

[The "church doors" are opened, and there are no people/fingers inside.]

Actor: The Boom was over. Throughout the 1960s, membership dropped. The United Church considered the possibility of another union. This time with the Anglicans.

[Music: a sensual tango. As the actor describes the process of union negotiations in sultry tones, a United Church dancer and an Anglican Church dancer parallel the process with a dramatic flamenco/tango-style dance.]

Actor: For more than a decade, the discussion and debates went on: 29% of Anglicans, and more than half the United Church were eager for a union.

[The dancers move towards each other, circling each other.]

Actor: Meanwhile, 6% of "Uniteds" and 31% of Anglicans said they would leave the church if union became a reality.

[The dancers move apart. They go back and forth, pursuing and retreating.]

Actor: Would the United Church join a union with the Anglicans? …Yes! Yes, it would, said General Council.

[The United Church dancer reaches out to the Anglican dancer. The Anglican dancer circles the United Church dancer.]

Actor: And the Anglicans? Would they be willing? In 1975 the General Synod met and decided…

[The Anglican dancer starts to reach for the United Church dancer, and then, with a flick of the wrist, turns away.]

Actor: No! It flung the proposed union back in the United Church's face with a haughty laugh, turned its back, and danced off in its own direction.

[The Anglican Church dancer dances off, leaving the United Church dancer sad and dejected.]

Actor: The poor United Church. Disappointed and demoralized. United? Ha! It was a failure. The whole church, a failure!

[Another dancer enters and approaches the United Church dancer.]

Actor: But wait! Union is not an impossibility. The Evangelical United Brethren has been waiting in the wings since 1925, realizing only now that union with the United Church is its life's destiny. But can the United Church take another chance on union? Is it willing to risk being burned yet again?

[A moment of hesitation, then the two dancers mesh into a tango.]

Actor: Yes! Yes! A smooth and beautiful union. "This is an easy way for the United Church to gain 10,000 members," said the overjoyed United Church.

[The EUB dancer dips the UC dancer.]

Actor: The Evangelical United Brethren, with an impish glint in its eye, replies, "No, it's an easy way for the EUB to gain a million."

[They dance off.]

SCENE 12: GOD IN A DRESS?!

[Ms. Curmudgeon storms in.]

Curmudgeon: Apparently, I'm not allowed to say "Father" anymore? No "King of Kings and Lord of Lords"? I can't even say "Mankind." Who do they think they are, taking my God, the God I have loved and prayed to my entire life, and changing Him into some sort of Mother/Father hybrid God?

Just the other day, in the middle of worship, I opened my hymnbook to find words crossed out. In a hymnbook! Words crossed out and new ones penciled in! That *must* be some kind of sin; I don't know what kind, but it must be some kind! God in a dress, what a ridiculous idea! I won't stand for it! I can't stand for it! I'm leaving the church. This is the last you'll see of me.

[She storms out.]

SCENE 13: ECUMENICAL DECADE OF WHO IN SOLIDARITY WITH WHAT?

[A couple of men come to center stage. A few women stand at the sides.]

Man 1: Throughout the 1970s and '80s, there was a growing awareness of the unequal status given to women in the church.

Woman 1: We'd been ordaining women since 1936…

Man 2: [obliviously cutting her off] Yet women in ordained ministry were still a minority. Men continued to be at center stage, wielding power and influence, while women remained at the margins.

Woman 2: Yay for the men!

Man 1: In many places in society and throughout the world, women were treated as second-class citizens. The political and economic oppression of women around the world was, and is, an injustice needing to be confronted.

Woman 1: Throughout the 20th century, women have worked to make their voices heard…

Man 2: [enthusiastically cutting her off] Yes, at times women had to be quite vocal in order to be acknowledged and treated as equals. Feminism within the church challenged us all to strive for gender equality in our practices, our relationships, our language, our theology, and our structures. And, in turn, the church became a voice calling for justice and gender equality in the world.

Woman 1: But…

Man 1: Yes, but it still seemed that men held a monopoly on positions of power. In society and in the church.

[Woman 1 pushes her way into center stage. The other women join her. The men move to the side.]

Woman 1: In 1988, churches around the world committed themselves to an Ecumenical Decade of Churches in Solidarity with Women. It was an opportunity for people of faith to explore issues of gender justice, to challenge long-standing power dynamics, to re-imagine God and our relation to the holy, and to celebrate the role of women in the church and in the world. It was an opportunity for women to finally take center stage.

Woman 2: The Ecumenical Decade provided many wonderful opportunities, although at times there was concern that the advances being made would never have any real impact on the mainstream church, that the Ecumenical Decade of Churches in Solidarity with Women was, in fact, an Ecumenical Decade of *Women* in Solidarity with Women.

Man 2: [moving back into the center] Now that's not fair. I'm a man and I'm very supportive of the Decade. I ran a study group on women of the Bible.

Man 1: And I seconded various anti-sexism motions at presbytery.

[As the men excitedly share their experiences, the women move off to the side.]

Man 2: I helped raise money to start a shelter for abused women.

Man 1: And I started a men's group, where we can talk about our emotions, because when men really begin to understand themselves emotionally…

Man 2: And the way they have been socialized into certain ways of acting in the world…

Man 1: Yes! When men finally have a chance to deal with their own issues, it makes for more mutual and open relationships between men and women.

[The men are once again at center stage, with the women on the sides.]

Woman 2: Yay for the men!

Woman 1: You know, I can't even begin to tell you what's wrong with this picture.

[Woman 1 leaves.]

Man 2: When are we going to have a Decade in Solidarity with *Men*?

Woman 1: [from offstage, frustrated] You've had the last 500!

Man 1: I think she has issues.

Man 2: She should express herself more.

[The men and remaining women leave.]

SCENE 14: THE APOLOGY

[A bare stage. The sound of a telephone ringing, and then the click of an answering machine starting. A recorded voice is heard.]

Voice: Hi, you've reached the First Nations people of Canada. We can't come to the phone right now, so please leave your apology at the sound of the tone… For example, "Long before your people journeyed to this land, our people were here," etc, etc.… Anyway, we'll be in and out throughout the week, but we will be checking for apologies on a regular basis. If you've already left an apology, thank you very much. Our people will contact your people, and…we'll get back to you. Megwitch.

[The sound of a beep is heard.]

SCENE 15: SAY WHAT?

[A game show host and four contestants, two teams of two, enter.]

Host: Hi folks, welcome back to Canada's favorite game show, *Say What?* Throughout the game our two teams have been evenly matched. This is the round that will decide it all. Are the contestants ready? Then put on your headphones.

[One member of each team puts on headphones.]

Host: While Terry and Doug are listening to the Mini-Pops singing *Guide Me, O Thou Great Jehovah* again and again and again, I'll let Ruth and Wilbur know their topic. Ruth, Wilbur, you have to get your partners to guess the phrase "Issues the United Church has taken a stand on," without using the words "issue," "united," "church," "taken," "stand," or "on." Are you ready? Wilbur, you get to go first.

[Wilbur's partner, Doug, takes off his headphones and sits opposite Wilbur.]

Wilbur: OK, um, these are things, things, statements that, um, um, you know, like gambling, or substance abuse, sexual harassment, pornography…

Doug: Things to do in Etobicoke on a Friday night.

Wilbur: No. No, bigger. Like disarmament, human rights, capital punishment, aboriginal concerns and land rights…

Doug: Things you read about in a newspaper?

Wilbur: Close. These are things that…some people…might want to have a say about. Like agriculture, immigration, refugees, collective bargaining, the economy…

Doug: Things that…my mother wouldn't let us talk about at the dinner table?

[A buzzer sounds.]

Host: I'm sorry, your time is up. Let's see if Ruth and Terry fare any better. Do you remember the topic, Ruth? Then begin.

[Terry takes her headphones off and sits opposite Ruth.]

Ruth: Sex.

[Slight pause.]

Terry: Issues the United Church has taken a stand on?

Ruth: That's correct.

Host: Wow, very impressive. Good work, Terry and Ruth. You'll come back next week for our tournament of champions. Wilbur and Doug, we have some lovely parting gifts for you. Tune in next time, folks, for everyone's favorite game show, *Say What?*

[The contestants and the host leave.]

SCENE 16: ROMEO AND 88

[Enter a narrator (Chorus).]

Chorus: In 1988, a report was put before the General Council of the United Church proposing that homosexual orientation should not bar people from consideration for ministry.

[Ms. Curmudgeon storms in, furious. So furious, in fact, that she can't speak. After a blustery moment, she storms out again.]

A trumpet fanfare is played, and two groups enter, taking opposite sides of the stage. One group is "For." The person speaking for this group carries a microphone labeled "1." A young woman named Julie is part of this group. The other group is "Against." The person speaking for this second group carries a microphone labeled "2." A young man named Romeo is part of this group. The scene is performed in Shakespearean style.]

Chorus: Two factions, both alike in certainty,

in fair Victoria, where we lay our scene,

from ancient grudge – debate and disagree,

in terms at times polite, at times obscene.

Two microphones, one *for*, one *'gainst*, and see,

a chasm untraversable between.

For: In faith, we do *affirm* the right of all –

it matters not if they be straight or gay –

to be ordained if fit they be, and thus

to mike the first we come to have our say.

Against: We needs must voice *concern,* lest Bible law

and Christian values all be left behind.

We love the sinner, hate the sin, thus we

to mike the second come to speak our mind.

Romeo: From forth these sep'rate camps of Aye and Nay

a pair of star-crossed lovers step apart.

Julie: And whilst in council rancor holds its sway,

these two pass resolutions of the heart.

Chorus: For prelude to our tale seek '81.

A woman – lesbian and self-declared –

feels she, by Conference of Hamilton,

should be ordained. This feeling is not shared.

And thus ignites a decade of debate:

Should gays and lesbians from pulpit preach?

And here, at Gen'ral Council '88,

the church must needs a resolution reach.

Against: Wouldst thou malign and undermine the faith?

For: Wouldst thou further oppress the trodden down?

Against: And wouldst thou disregard the moral law?

For: And wouldst thou catapult us back in time

to days of silence, closets, and of death?

Chorus: At times beneath discussion and debate

lurk undertones of anger, fear, and hate.

Against: Thou rabble-rouser!

For: Thou comfortable pew-sitter!

Against: Thou reveler in perversion!

For: Thou sexually repressed Bible-thumping dinosaur!

Against: Thou Sunday school corrupter!

For: Thou homophobe!

Against: Thou faggot!

For: Thou fascist!

Against: Fie!

For: Fie on thee!

Against: Fie on thee!

[The "For" and "Against" sides start to advance towards each other. Romeo and Julie push forward and stand between.]

Julie: Hold! Pray, halt thy advance, I do implore.

Forsake thine enmity and let us speak.

Romeo: Pour oil upon thy calumny, I pray.

Clasp hands and speak thy diff'rences as friends,

for here, across the council floor, have I

found one who sets my soul afire with love.

[Romeo and Julie clasp hands.]

Julie: And likewise have I found true love at last!

In troth, our love needs be confess'd and known,

that whilst our elders resolutions pass'd,

in secret we made passes of our own;

whilst tabled motions did distract the court,

emotions led us under tables to consort.

For: This cannot be, for we are of mike one,

whilst they and all their kind speak at mike two!

Romeo: Thou, Julie, art the basis of my union, and

all 20 articles of faith to me!

Julie: And thou, Romeo, my inclusive church!

[The leader of the "For" group starts to pull Julie away.]

For: Julie, enough! We will no more of this.

Julie: Oh, Romeo, Romeo, wherefore art thou C.O.C.?

Romeo: Halt, gentles, heed. And, pray ye, watch awhile,

as we, two star-crossed lovers, by our faith

unite two camps through dialogue and grace.

Julie: We shall by pure example make amends

transforming bitter rivals into friends.

[Romeo and Julie take the microphones and move towards each other in slow motion, reaching out to each other.]

Against: What foolishness is this? ...Alas! Alack!

Don't bring those mikes so close or they'll...

[As Romeo and Julie come close to each other the microphones feedback. The "For" and "Against" sides grab their ears. Romeo and Julie collapse. The sound dies down, and the two groups gather around the bodies of Romeo and Julie.]

Against: Oh woe, and what a sorry sight is this.

For: It grieves my heart to see them so undone.

Against: Come, let us bear them hence from here. We shall

speak more of this anon… anon… anon.

For: Hie we hence, to ruminate

upon this, "the issue"…and the 88.

[They carry Romeo and Julie out.]

Chorus: General Council '88 drafted a resolution declaring that full membership in the church was open to all people, regardless of sexual preference, who professed faith in Jesus Christ and obedience to him, and left the power to decide who should be ordained where it had always been, with the congregations, presbyteries, and conferences.

SCENE 17: FRACZILLA

[A narrator does a dramatic voice-over.]

Narrator: The United Church had once again survived trial by fire, but the ripple effects of this latest conflict were felt well into the '90s. Long-standing theological and philosophical differences had been exposed, and the years following 1988 were known informally as "the years of walking on eggshells." The storm of conflict had subsided, *but for how long?*

[The following scene is performed with one group of actors acting on stage while another group on the side provides the dialogue, creating the effect of a poorly dubbed Japanese monster movie. A military General and a Scientist enter.]

General: Doctor, I must speak with you.

Scientist: What? Who is there? Oh, it is you, General Public.

General: Our sonar has detected an enormous mass lurking in the bay.

Scientist: Yes, my instruments have also indicated the same thing. Our modern high-tech computers are analyzing the data.

[A computer, or even just a person in a cardboard box, spits out a punch card. The Scientist looks at it.]

Scientist: Aha, as I suspected. The worrisome presence hiding beneath the surface is the specter of divisive conflict in the church.

General: [frightened] Oh no! What if it rises from the bay and engulfs us?!

Scientist: Do not panic!

> [The Scientist slaps the General. If you'd like, have one of the dubbing actors provide the sound of the slap either before or after the slap is acted out.]

Scientist: This creature feeds on conflict, therefore we must avoid all signs of conflict, difference, or division. We are one church, after all.

General: Yes, I agree. We must do nothing that will cause us to argue or disagree. Unity and harmony at all costs.

Scientist: What shall we do, then?

General: Not fight.

Scientist: Yes, obviously not fight, but what else?

> [Pause.]

General: We could watch TV.

Scientist: Yes, television will distract us from the specter of denominational conflict.

> [The Scientist pulls out a remote control and turns on the TV. A Jeopardy-like board appears on the screen. The game show Host and a contestant, Bill Phipps, enter.]

Scientist: Ah, a North American game show. This should be good for a laugh.

> [The Scientist and the General put their hands on their hips and laugh. "Ha ha ha." Then they turn their attention to the game show, which is not dubbed.]

Host: Welcome back to Moderator Jeopardy, brought to you by the editorial board of the *Ottawa Citizen*. Today's moderator contestant is the Right Reverend Bill Phipps. Reverend Phipps, your categories are "Canadian Economic Policies," "Transnational Corporations," "The Effect of Declining Social Spending," and "Political Activism in the '90s."

Phipps: I'll take "Canadian Economic Policy" for 400, Alex.

Host: All right, under "Canadian Economic Policy" …The answer is "Your view on the bodily resurrection of Jesus Christ."

Phipps: Uh… You're sure this is the right category?

Host: "Canadian Economic Policy" for 400. "Your view on the bodily resurrection of Jesus Christ." We need an answer, Reverend Phipps.

Phipps: Well…if what you're asking is, do I believe in a literal interpretation of the gospel story and a physical resuscitation of a dead body, I'd probably have to say no, but…

Host: I'm sorry, that's not the correct answer, nor is it phrased in the form of a question.

Phipps: But...

Host: Perhaps you can make up the points in the Double Jeopardy round. Would you like to try "Transnational Corporations" for 100?

> [The game show Host and Phipps leave, the screen returns to blank. The focus returns to the dubbed Scientist and General.]

Scientist: Oh, he should not have said that.

General: No, it is good that he said that. That is what I have always thought.

Scientist: He is the moderator of the United Church. It is not what the church believes!

General: It is what I believe, and I am the church as much as you are!

Scientist: If *that* is what you believe, maybe you aren't the church at all!

General: Oh yeah?

> [A roaring sound is heard.]

Scientist: What is that sound?

General: Oh no, what have we done! Look! The monster is rising from the bay! It is enormous!

Scientist: Run! Run for your lives! Flee from the wrath of – Fraczilla!

> [A shadow puppet or a poorly drawn overhead of a sharp-toothed tyrannosaurus-like monster appears on the screen. Sound of roaring. The Scientist and the General run around, pointing and screaming.]

General: Aaiiii! It will destroy the church!

Scientist: We're doomed!!

General: Doomed!

> [A Hero enters, also dubbed.]

Hero: You people there! Why are you running about? The new millennium is upon us, and we must prepare.

General: But Fraczilla...!

Hero: Cowards! We must not run and hide from Fraczilla. We must confront Fraczilla, for that is the only way that we can move into the future, to be a relevant church in this modern world.

Scientist: But our numbers are shrinking. People have left the church.

Hero: You are foolish people! I have no time for you. The church was not formed to worry for its own survival, but to bring justice, compassion, and salvation to the world.

General: But that means facing up to Fraczilla, and Fraczilla is very big and scary!

Hero: We will face Fraczilla together. Are you with me?

Scientist and General: Yes, yes, we are with you.

Hero: Then, to the future!

[The Hero rushes off towards Fraczilla. The Scientist and General wait.]

Scientist: I hope he makes it.

General: Me too.

[The General and the Scientist sneak off in the opposite direction.]

SCENE 18: THE BIG BLOCKBUSTER FINALE PRODUCTION NUMBER

[An actor enters.]

Actor 1: Now, this is the scene I've been waiting the whole show for. This is the big blockbuster finale production number, where we pull together everything from the last 75 years of the United Church and propel it with faith and hope into the future. This is where we get to act out our vision of mission for the church. We're going to bring in our global partners in ministry from around the world, and hold up all the wonderful possibilities for new projects here in Canada.

[Another actor enters and stands by, waiting for Actor 1 to finish.]

Actor 1: This is where we tie in the importance of youth and children, and the contributions of the various ethnic ministries in the United Church. And express our hopes for how the church can respond to a world of environmental degradation, multinationals, and ethnic cleansing. And share a vision of ways the church could be meaningful and relevant in a world of Internet and computer technology, and, and... Wow! There's just so much that we've packed into this scene! I'm *so* excited! I'm been looking forward to this scene since we started the play, and now, finally...

Actor 2: Scene's been canceled.

Actor 1: What?

Actor 2: Ran out of money.

Actor 1: What!?

Actor 2: Blew it all on special effects for the Fraczilla scene.

[Actor 1 is shocked and stunned.]

Actor 1: Special effects?! You mean that cheesy dinosaur thing?!

Actor 2: That "cheesy dinosaur thing," as you call it, was completely digitally rendered. Do you know how hard it is to mat that kind of C.G.I. in with live actors so it looks realistic?

Actor 1: [frustrated] So, what, you're saying we don't get to do our big blockbuster finale production number about the mission of the church?

Actor 2: Pretty much.

Actor 1: Because of budget constraints.

Actor 2: 'Fraid so.

Actor 1: How are we supposed to end the play?

Actor 2: Well, I've been thinking that since it's a play about the history of the United Church, and since, you know, the United Church is *still going*, maybe the play shouldn't have an ending.

Actor 1: That's stupid. There needs to be some sort of ending. Something to wrap things up.

Actor 2: Yeah, well, the other thing is…we've just about used up our budget for script too.

Actor 1: …We've used up our budget for script?

Actor 2: We can only afford a couple more lines and then we run out.

Actor 1: And once the script runs out, then what?

[Actor 2 opens his mouth to speak, but has run out of script. Actor 1 waits for a reply. Actor 2 shrugs apologetically. The two of them stand, awkwardly, not knowing what to do next. Eventually Actor 1 walks off, frustrated. A short pause. Actor 2 smiles apologetically at the audience and starts to leave as well. Actor 1 returns, writing furiously on a large cue card. Actor 1 holds up the cue card for Actor 2. Actor 2 reads.]

Actor 2: "Oh, good idea… Since 1925 the United Church of Canada has tried to do the will of God. It has not always agreed on what that will is, but it has struggled faithfully with the difficult task of living Christ's message in the world. And it will continue to do so. So that all maybe one."

[Actor 2 checks the spelling with Actor 1.]

Actor 2: Maybe one?

[Actor 1 makes a correction with a quick stroke.]

Actor 2: May be one.

[Actor 1 and Actor 2 nod to each other and leave. The end.]

APPENDIX

List of Characters

I usually prefer not to list all the characters at the beginning of a play, but sometimes (for example, when casting) it is useful to have a complete reference list before you. Please remember: some of these plays were written to be "multi-cast" (i.e. one actor may play different parts).

STRANGE ANGELS
Joe
Karl
Marsha

DOG EAT DOG WORLD
Rufus
Fido
Rev. Whiskers
Human

A FAIR TRADE
Jesus Morales (*hey-zoos mo-rah-lays*)
Mildred
Walter
Workers: at least 5 of them
(Workers also play, Co-op Worker, Shipper, Roaster, Retailer, and Consumer)

DAVID'S RULE

SCENE 1
Storyteller/Han
David
Jesse
Samuel
Saul
Israelite soldiers
Goliath
Philistine soldiers

SCENE 2
Storyteller/Witch of Endor
David
Jonathan
Saul
Band of prophets
Prophet

DAVID'S RULE cont'd

SCENE 2 CONT'D
Exiles (5)
Soldier
Messenger

SCENE 3
Storyteller/Nathan
David
Joab
Bathsheba
Uriah the Hittite
Rich Man
Poor Man
Visitor
Lamb

SCENE 4
Storyteller
David
Amnon
Tamar
Absalom
Solomon
Joab
Soldiers 1 and 2

SCENE 5
Storyteller/Witch of Endor/Hannah/Han/Nathan
David
Solomon
Samuel
Saul
Servant
Jesse
Wise women 1 and 2
Tamar

WORK
Matthew
Shelby
Ian
Sarah
Gwen

JUST 'CAUSE
Bride
Mom
Minister

LEGEND OF SAINT ANDREW
Actor
Apostles, including
Peter
Bartholomew
Thomas
Matthias
Andrew
King Zeuxippos
Resurrected people from the sea
Scythian Mayor
Scythian townspeople (at least five)
Demon dog/Consultant
Traveler
Pregnant Woman
Angel
Cannibal
Soldier
Aegeus

TABLES TURNED AND THE STONE GETS ROLLED AWAY
Mary/Jesus
Micah/moneychanger
Esther/high priest

A PRAIRIE NATIVITY
Gabriel
Angel Choir (audience)
Mary
Farmers 1 and 2
Waitress

MAYBE ONE?

SCENE 1: IN THE BEGINNING
Actors 1 and 2

SCENE 2: UNION NIGHT IN CANADA
Ron McCain
Dawn Sherry
George Pidgeon
Ephraim Scott
Samuel Chown
Church-Union players
Anti-Union players
Referee

SCENE 3: BASIS OF UNION COUNTDOWN
U.C. Casem

SCENE 4: CONTROVERSY!
Ms. Curmudgeon

SCENE 5: THE PUNCH AND NELLIE SHOW
Punch
Nellie McClung
Voice-over

SCENE 6: THE DEPRESSION
Patient

SCENE 7: THE FEARLESS MIDGET
Army Chaplain

SCENE 8: INTERNMENT
Tak Komiyama
Patient
Chaplain

SCENE 9: THE ENDICOTT ZONE
Narrator
Dad
Mom
Daughter
Son
Reverend Bob
James Endicott